ACCESS, OPPORTUNITY, AND SUCCESS

ACCESS, OPPORTUNITY, AND SUCCESS

Keeping The Promise of Higher Education

Martha E. Casazza
Laura Bauer

PRAEGER

Westport, Connecticut
London

Library of Congress Cataloging-in-Publication Data

Casazza, Martha E., 1947–
  Access, opportunity, and success : keeping the promise of higher education /
Martha E. Casazza and Laura Bauer.
      p.   cm.
  Includes bibliographical references and index.
  ISBN 0–275–98965–8 (alk. paper)
  1. Education, Higher—United States.   2. College students—United States.   I.
Bauer, Laura.   II. Title.
  LA227.4.C37   2006
  378.73—dc22   2005025489

British Library Cataloguing in Publication Data is available.

Library of Congress Catalog Card Number: 2005025489
ISBN: 0–275–98965–8

First published in 2006

Praeger Publishers, 88 Post Road West, Westport, CT 06881
An imprint of Greenwood Publishing Group, Inc.
www.praeger.com

Printed in the United States of America

The paper used in this book complies with the
Permanent Paper Standard issued by the National
Information Standards Organization (Z39.48–1984).

10 9 8 7 6 5 4 3 2 1

❧ CONTENTS

PREFACE

We regularly hear from the media and our legislators about the state of education in the United States. They create a great deal of attention by declaring that too much money is spent on education, and that funding should be put into activities that have more direct, concrete outcomes. We hear all the time about the reduction in academic standards and the fact that too many students who are not adequately prepared are entering colleges and universities. Everyone points the finger at everyone else: College instructors like to blame high school teachers who, in turn, attribute the blame to the elementary school teachers, who look to the families and allege that there is not enough support at home. Meanwhile, the general public blames educators as a whole for a system that does not seem to be delivering on its promises.

What are those promises anyway? Is it that everyone who aspires to have a college degree be given a chance? Is it providing financial aid to those who want to attend college but cannot afford it? Is it ensuring that public schools in urban areas are supported sufficiently to guarantee adequate preparation for college? Is it creating academic support systems along the way to assist those who need additional help to maximize their potential?

Whatever the promises, more students than ever before are entering college today without a sufficient academic foundation, and many of them are succeeding. There are many reasons for their success including individual commitment and persistence along with a network of dedicated educators and parents who believed in them and helped them navigate the often complicated educational system. These individuals have stories to tell that are rarely heard in the media, and it is these stories that unfold in this book.

We conducted dozens of interviews for this oral history in order to ensure that these often unheard stories from within the educational system are passed on to the future generations. These stories demonstrate the power of promises kept and doors opened. Behind the hallowed walls of higher education are students who did not grow up expecting to attend college, students who walked through open doors not knowing what to expect on the other side. For many, these open doors became revolving doors, and they simply gave up. For many others though, there were unexpected successes, successes that included more than academic accomplishments. For those who met their goals, the degree or the certificate was only a part of the achievement. They came through the system with increased self-confidence that would empower them in the world beyond college.

Student voices are powerful, but alone they would only be a part of the whole story. There were teachers and administrators who understood the world of these students. Often they had come from similar backgrounds as the students, and they wanted to provide opportunities for others. They created systems of support and wrote policies that would enable more students to reach their maximum potential. It is these stories that we want to tell side by side with those of the students. It is this combination that comprises the oral history documented in this book, a history that will inform readers about the power of promises kept.

We have chosen to record this unique perspective on American higher education from the inside out and in the first person. We feel it is through this voice that the stories come alive. Where it seemed helpful to provide a context, we included appropriate references. For the most part, however, we let the interviewees speak for themselves. Where else can you read the following words of a recognized leader in the field, Hunter R. Boylan?

> Meanwhile the street gangs were out there with no resources whatsoever. They were always having activities, organizing things, were pretty highly motivated and they communicated well. And, they were very effective at what they were doing. In fact, they were much more effective at being street gang members than college students were at being college students. And so I thought, "... you know these guys have all the characteristics they need for success except for the opportunity to attend college."

It is insights like this one, and the subsequent outcomes, that are too often lost. Unlike traditional research paradigms and theoretical frameworks, informal stories are often not recorded, and we lose a significant source of knowledge. This knowledge base can enrich our practice and lead to a broader perspective for future generations as they create policies and try to understand how to make the educational system more relevant for an increasingly diverse society.

ORGANIZATION AND THEMES

When we first began the interviews for this history, we identified groups of individuals who we felt needed to be represented: "pioneers" who envisioned early on how to open the educational doors effectively; "leaders" in the professional associations, who emerged during the 1960s and 1970s to provide a network for those on the front lines, working with students; "practitioners," who met and worked with the then-nontraditional students and developed strategies to maximize their potential, and the "students" themselves, who often entered the system not knowing what to expect. We originally thought that these stories should be organized into separate sections according to the different categories. We expected to hear different perspectives that would provide, in the end, an overall story. What we found, however, was entirely different. As we continued the interviews, it became increasingly apparent that there were similar themes emerging across the categories. It would have been an artificial division to separate the stories. As we began organizing them side by side, the messages became powerful; a student often expressed the same perspective as a pioneer. For instance, Calvin Mackie, who was placed into a remedial reading course in college and subsequently received a PhD in Mechanical Engineering, told us,

In college I had a teacher and the great thing about this teacher was that he always challenged me and he started calling me "doctor." And you know people talk about speaking into an existence and he pushed me and pushed me and said, "We expect you to go for your highest degree." I had never even heard of a PhD when I entered college.

In another interview, Martha Maxwell, a pioneer in the area of conceptualizing the meaning of learning assistance for all students, was describing herself as a professional to us.

Cheerleader ought to be included. I would say that, in describing myself, perennial student and cheerleader are the most apt descriptions. We are dealing with students who come from backgrounds where success has not been part of their repertoire. They have not been encouraged; in fact, many of them have been discouraged in academia, so they don't feel they can do it. Once you get them working, then I think you have to be a cheerleader and help them along the way.

These two excerpts helped lead us to the first theme in this oral history—the power in having a belief in students. The reader will discover that this is expressed in various ways. Students frequently identified individuals, from their early years and through college, who believed in their ability to succeed in the educational system. Administrators and practitioners, in demonstrating their belief in students, often advocated for mandatory institutional systems and challenges that they felt would help students find their way. Others expressed the need to build personal relationships with students and to develop a more nurturing approach to assist students.

The second theme describes the struggle between granting access to those who may be underprepared for postsecondary education while still maintaining standards of excellence at colleges and universities. For many who are not directly involved in providing services to students who need additional learning assistance, there is little question that these two concepts, access and standards, are diametrically opposed. They will argue that by allowing underprepared students in the door, one is automatically lowering the academic standards of the institution. But in our interviews, we found that for those who believe in students and in opening access, there is an adamant assertion that access and standards belong together. Without standards and learning assistance programs, students may be admitted in the name of access but they will soon leave or create frustrations in the classroom, because no one has advised them or worked with them to ensure that they are prepared to meet the standards. Robert McCabe, former president of Miami-Dade Community College, says,

I think the two most important planks in the whole concept, well actually more help was certainly necessary and more intervention, was limiting classes, limiting loads for people who weren't doing well, and also not letting anyone proceed into courses for which they weren't prepared. Now, at the same time most institutions did make that move in the 1970s, and the result was a growing failure. In other words, we admitted people . . . and then we did not help them gain the competencies they needed for proceeding into content courses. We put them in places where they were doomed to fail.

He goes on to talk about how his institution developed policies to facilitate the success of students in access programs by mandating adherence to a set of academic standards.

The third theme we discovered is the importance of institutional commitment to creating and supporting access and the integration of support services into the mainstream of the institution's mission and purpose. Individuals and programs that deliver support services to students must be valued at the institution from the top down and not relegated to a secondary status. Frequently, in order to receive this recognition and status, practitioners must be proactive and prepared to demonstrate successful outcomes far more readily than their colleagues in more traditional departments or units. Karen Patty-Graham, a learning center director at Southern Illinois University, shared with us the frustrations of working with an administrator who was not committed to her program.

> Administrators make a real difference. The bad ones look at our students as dummies and even refer to them in such terms. They imply and overtly state that our instructors are no more than glorified high school teachers. This type of administrator doesn't provide support emotionally, intellectually, or financially for the program and filters the information that gets up to the provost level. I have had to continually try to prove that what we are doing is worthwhile. I knew that if I could show that our students were successful in the university, there was no way he was going to be able to eliminate our students or our program from the university. I had to really try to disseminate that information as widely as I could . . . and I also found ways to remind him that if we weren't here, a third to a half of the freshman class wouldn't be here.

On the other side of the administrative coin are the comments of Santiago Silva, former vice president of Student Services and Development at South Texas Community College. He says,

> Students are coming into our institutions ill prepared already. This (placement into developmental courses) just simply adds to the frustration level that our students experience. It is one more blow to their self-esteem. Many of them get so frustrated and discouraged because they cannot pass the developmental education courses. They leave our institutions feeling more defeated than they felt when they entered. We need to continue to improve our instructional materials as well as the curriculum. We need to become more innovative in identifying strategies that can be incorporated into our curriculum that will assist our students in succeeding. This would obviously increase our retention

rates and impact our graduation/completion rates and, at least, minimize the revolving-door phenomenon.

The final theme that emerged from our research is the significance of having a purposeful repertoire of strategies that provides the support necessary for students to succeed. The most effective strategies are those that encompass the whole student. They not only address strengthening of the basic academic skills related to reading, writing, and mathematics needed across the curriculum, but also the student's level of self-esteem. It is difficult to separate these two aspects of an individual struggling to succeed. The skills are necessary but without a commensurate increase in self-confidence, the student is likely to continue experiencing difficulty. Milton "Bunk" Spann, a pioneer in the field of student development, described a strategy, reality counseling, that he found successful with students.

> I think it was effective because it again addressed the issue, in a very practical way, the issue of whole person development. We not only were involved in teaching students basic skills, but we were involved in working with and helping them to realize their worth and dignity....We even talked with them about some of the various sophisticated strategies that they used to fail and suggested to them that the same intelligence might be applied to succeeding. And so we began to outline, in consultation with them, strategies for succeeding in a particular course or perhaps in some life area that they were struggling with.

David Taylor, former dean of the General College at the University of Minnesota, also spoke of the significance of reaching out to students through a range of delivery models.

> Being able to lecture is not enough. We have to be able to know about learning styles in order to approach people with different learning styles so that everyone can grasp the profundity of what we're putting in front of them in ways that are consistent with their abilities. Then we need to offer a variety of ways to reinforce that learning.

Many of these themes overlap and, in the chapters that follow, the reader will see how close the interrelationships truly are. We acknowledge that some of the stories could easily fit into several categories, but we have organized them into a coherent history that makes sense to us. We have also done our best to keep the voices authentic in order for the reader to really *hear* the stories as they were told to us. For that reason, we have kept the interview portions of the book informal and, for the most part, have not adjusted the language to follow a formal grammatical structure. Also in the interest of archiving a representative historical record, we have not altered either the language or the contents of the stories to reflect our own views.

TERMINOLOGY

There are so many terms related to educational access and student support systems that it seems important to define a few of them in order for the stories in this book to make sense. We will also describe some of the controversies surrounding various terms. Many of the terms are pejorative, and professionals involved in the field are continuously trying to find ways to describe their work by using terms that have the least negative connotation.

In 1991 (Rubin), a group of professionals in higher education defined programs/services labeled "learning assistance" and "developmental education," both of which are heard throughout the interviews, often interchangeably. Although they are defined in different words, the underlying concept is similar: to improve student performance. Developmental education is frequently described as a process, a subdiscipline of psychology and a field of research, of teaching and practice. Learning assistance, on the other hand, is talked about more in terms of activities and programs developed to facilitate student success directly. Professionals who practice within a learning center where services do not include coursework refer to their work as learning assistance; whereas, those who deliver formal courses more often call themselves developmental educators.

Professional associations have developed over the years to provide networks for specific categories of practitioners, although membership is open to all groups. The National Association for Developmental Education (NADE) provides professional development and annual conferences primarily for developmental educators while the National Tutoring Association (NTA), the College Reading and Learning Association (CRLA), and the National College Learning Center Association (NCLCA) focus on practitioners who are more often found in college and university learning centers.

Beyond the terms used to define the professionals who provide assistance and support to students are the general labels ascribed to the programs. There has been a gradual change in this terminology, which has indicated a shifting perspective toward the underprepared student. Through the early 1960s, the term "remedial" was most often heard. It implied a more limited approach and primarily described programs that focus on correcting specific skill deficits. It was reflective of a medical model approach to learning assistance in which treatments were prescribed for discrete symptoms with little consideration given to the whole "patient" (Clowes 1980).

By the 1970s, the term "compensatory" was used interchangeably with "remedial." Compensatory became popular following equal rights legislation that funded programs designed to help students make up for earlier discrimination and poverty (Casazza & Silverman 1996). Both remedial and compensatory are terms that contributed to a negative connotation of programs and students. They tend to focus on weaknesses and highlight the differences between these students and those enrolled in more advanced coursework.

The more recent term, "developmental," came from the field of college student personnel and from the beginning applied to programs that took a comprehensive view of individuals and provided support for growth in both academic and personal areas. This approach assumes that everyone has talents that need to be acknowledged while weaker areas are developed. This supposedly conveys a more positive perspective to students who need assistance (Casazza & Silverman 1996).

We asked our interviewees for their thoughts on the various labels and definitions that have been applied over the years. Most of them felt that the current language sent a negative message but were not sure there was much that could be done to change that message. Jane Neuburger shared,

> Do you remember the red birds and the blue birds? Whatever we call ourselves, some people are still going to see us as the red birds...the red bird reading group. Whatever you label it, the students are going to know that's the group that is not doing so well. We could change our name to anything, and it would still be clear that the work we do is primarily with underprepared students.

Dana Britt Lundell stated her concern that the term developmental was too often applied to individuals and led to faulty assumptions.

> For me, the term still has an individual assumption about student learning. Many people are still saying, "Oh you know we don't need individual students like that in our programs." And that's the whole conversation that

gets going. I guess I like the word "access" better, and when I think about developmental education it does mean access and that helps me think about what I do. It's about creating opportunities along the continuum instead of placing barriers to student learning and to a postsecondary education. It's creating a whole institutional environment rather than just a single doorway for a single student to walk through.

Robin Remich also chooses to think about the term developmental in a more global way. She told us, "Everybody is a developmental student. Developmental education just means that everybody is starting at some point. Whatever that point is to them; they need to develop to the next point . . . we all become developmental students when we learn something new."

Gladys Shaw pointed out that the various terms do carry different connotations and also that being underprepared for college coursework has much to do with motivation and utilization of information.

I think remedial and compensatory are the most negative. Now, that may be a prejudice on my part. I don't know. Developmental, to me, is a much softer term. It seems to mean opportunities along the way; it's not putting a stigma on them. It's saying we know you can learn; you just have to learn in your own time. And we're all motivated at different times to do different things. When these kids first took these courses, chances are they didn't have a clue as to why they were taking them or what the impact would be if they didn't learn it well. And you know knowledge goes away if you don't use it. For example, if you asked me to go back and work some algebraic equations, I would be very developmental.

Santiago Silva sums up the positive connotation that practitioners are hoping for when they use the word developmental to describe their work.

It is a means with which an individual not only improves academically but personally. Feeling better about ourselves has an effect on our self-esteem. The self-esteem is strong and has a ripple effect on other things in a person's life. The challenge that we as educators face is helping students see developmental education as something that is positive. The negative connotation it has is interpreted as, "Something is wrong with us. We are not up to standards." The negative connotation that is associated with developmental education keeps our students from seeing these courses as a good thing. They see them as "dummy" courses and as a way of keeping them down.

When we talk about developmental students and the field of developmental studies, the most common response is "Huh? What does *that* mean exactly?" Educators, legislators, students, and the media are often confused about what the term developmental means in the context of underprepared students. They have no way of knowing that developmental education is a field of study based on theory and research, and that developmental students are not "slow" or "lacking" in ability. We are hopeful that this text will clear up some of the confusion and shed light on a significant component of our educational system.

We have chosen to begin the stories with a chapter devoted to a brief historical overview of what access to higher education looked like even before the twentieth century. Readers may be surprised to find that it crossed institutional boundaries and included not only community colleges but also elitist universities. Chapters 2 through 5 tell the stories and are organized by the themes we have identified here. In the final chapter, we have constructed a set of recommendations that we believe will help to keep the doors open in a meaningful way for those wishing to enter. These recommendations have taken shape through the stories we have recorded, and we believe they will contribute to keeping the promise of providing both access and excellence across our educational system.

✒ ACKNOWLEDGMENTS

An oral history project like this one cannot be successful without the help of many individuals, and we are truly indebted to so many of our students and colleagues for helping us make it happen. First, there were those who agreed to be interviewed. They spent many hours with us reflecting on their past experiences and providing us with the multiple lenses necessary to gain a comprehensive picture of this rich history. The first individual to be interviewed was Martha Maxwell. At that starting point, the plan was to videotape all interviews. For that to happen, Carol Eckermann and Martha Casazza spent three days living with Martha Maxwell in her Maryland apartment complex and arranging for video equipment. She was gracious enough to host us for nearly a week when a surprise snowstorm hit the area and stranded us. Following that first interview, Gerry Chodkowski at National-Louis University spent many weeks editing the videotape. The second videotape was done with Milton "Bunk" Spann, who agreed to come to one of our homes while Martha interviewed and Laura did the videotaping. Once again, Gerry Chodkowski worked diligently at editing the tapes.

After the second videotape, it became clear that this method was not efficient time-wise or financially. The videotapes are available and are stored in the Martha Maxwell Archival Collection at National-Louis University in Chicago. The remainder of the interviews were conducted and audiotaped either in a face-to-face format or by telephone. It took many hours of transcribing to make the text available for the next stage of the project. We deeply appreciate the diligence of Anna Pastore, Elke

Kleisch, and Deborah Childs as they listened to every word and did a superb job of transcription. In addition to her skill in transcription, Elke became our expert resource for questions related to format and style. Some of our graduate students also conducted a few of the interviews, and we would like to acknowledge them here: Dale Griffee, Glasetta Barksdale, and Deborah Williams contributed an important component to this work.

We received two grants to help support our work. We received the Brenda Pfaehler Professional Development Grant from the National College Learning Center Association (NCLCA) and a grant from the Center for Research on Developmental Education and Urban Literacy (CRDEUL). These grants helped us travel in order to conduct some of our interviews. We would be remiss not to mention all the copying and mailing done by Neacie Metcalf on our behalf. She never missed a deadline nor did she ever leave out a significant document that needed to be included.

Of course, without the committed individuals we interviewed, this oral history never would have been recorded. Our interviewees were passionate about this work and spent hours talking to us and helping us edit and revise the text. We are also indebted to our editor, Susan Slesinger, who first recognized the value of this history and shepherded us through the publication process.

Our colleagues at National-Louis University have been extremely supportive of our work. On those days when we simply closed our doors and said, "Keep Out. Interview in process," they not only stayed away but also often carried out our responsibilities. A special thanks goes to both Steve Thompson, associate dean, and Scipio A. Colin III, department chair, for their collegial support and understanding during this process.

Finally, we are grateful for the ongoing personal support we have received from those who continue to encourage and cheer us on. Chuck's excitement for this project equaled Laura's. Without "The Rock," Martha would never take a break nor see how taking the time to reflect helps to make sense of the world.

Chapter 1

Historical Framework ॐ

While this oral history covers the latter half of the twentieth century, colleges and universities in the United States have been making room for underprepared students ever since the early eighteenth century. Rarely has it been without conflict or tension related to standards and an examination of the purpose of higher education. This chapter will provide a framework primarily for the twentieth century, but a few references to earlier times will help the reader gain a perspective on the whole concept of opening the doors to higher education. We begin by briefly describing the early colleges whose primary model of education included the classical institutions of Europe. While they hoped to attract only a very elitist population of well-prepared males, this was not always possible nor was it embraced by everyone. We also discuss the impact of federal legislation on the evolving purpose and enrollments of higher education, and then we review the range of support systems that have been created in order to facilitate success for the no longer "new" students.

EARLY WHISPERS OF ACCESS

Back in the earliest days of higher education in the United States, colleges such as Harvard and Yale had the training of clergy, and the preservation and maintenance of the cultural norms brought from Europe as their primary mission. This mission was supported by statements such as one from a seventeenth-century Harvard commencement address where the speaker expressed appreciation for the university's Puritan founders;

otherwise, "the ruling class would have been subjected to mechanics, cobblers, and tailors, the gentry would have been overwhelmed by lewd fellows of the baser sort, the sewage of Rome, the dregs of an illiterate plebs which judgeth much from emotion, little from truth" (Brubacher & Rudy 1976, p. 10).

Unbeknownst to the commencement speaker, at Harvard in the seventeenth century, 10 percent of its students came from families of artisans, seamen, and servants. The university reserved places for poorer students whose tuition was paid either through work assignments or assessments made to wealthier students (Brubacher & Rudy 1976). To provide individual assistance during this period, Harvard developed a system of tutoring. The tutors were drawn from the ranks of the faculty and did not form a subordinate rank of the teaching staff (Brubacher & Rudy 1976, p. 268).

According to an anecdote from the 1830s, Ezra Cornell, founder of Cornell University, expressed concern that a large number of applicants were not passing the university's entrance exam. He was told that the students simply did not know enough to be admitted. Cornell asked why the faculty could not teach the students what they did not know, and the professor in charge of admissions replied that the faculty was not prepared to teach the alphabet. He added that if Cornell wanted the faculty to teach spelling, he should have founded a primary school and not a university (Brier 1984). Following this conversation, the rejected students were allowed to take the exam again. During this period, Cornell also had a committee on "doubtful cases" whose responsibility was to make decisions regarding marginal applications (Casazza & Silverman 1996).

Francis Wayland, president of Brown University, attempted to open university doors through the creation of a university extension division that would include classes taught by the faculty of Brown. He wanted the college to be the "center of intelligence for all classes." This program lasted until 1854 when "unmistakable evidence began to accumulate that the quality of the student body was deteriorating." This discovery also led to the perception that President Wayland had lowered the standards of the undergraduate degree with his innovative "partial" coursework that did not lead to a degree (Brubacher & Rudy 1976, p. 107).

The stated criteria for being qualified for higher education during the eighteenth and nineteenth centuries were quite simple: males with a proper family background. The pool of qualified students was not large, however, and colleges were forced to admit a wider range of students than they would have preferred. The president at Vassar College said during this period that, "the range of student achievement extends to a point lower than any scale could measure" (Brier 1984, p. 2).

In order to extend the opportunity for a higher education to a broader set of students, colleges like Amherst and Williams were founded for those who could not afford Harvard or Yale. These schools had the unfortunate effect of segregating the students who, because of their lesser means, were also less prepared. The students at Williams were described as "rough, brown featured, schoolmaster-looking, half-bumpkin, half-scholar, in black, ill-cut broadcloth" (Brubacher & Rudy 1976, p. 40).

In 1871, Harvard's president, Charles Eliot, lamented that freshmen entering Harvard demonstrated "bad spelling, incorrectness as well as inelegance of expression in writing, (and) ignorance of the simplest rules of punctuation." As a result, the university implemented an entrance exam that included an essay. By 1879, 50 percent of the applicants to Harvard were failing the exam and were admitted "on condition." This led the institution to provide academic assistance in order to further prepare the students for college-level classes (Weidner 1990, p. 4).

By the 1890s, educators at Harvard described a crisis among freshmen and formed a committee to examine the composition and rhetoric offerings at the college. The subsequent *Harvard Reports* linked the lack of writing skills to poor critical thinking and pointed the finger of blame at the lower educational levels. President Eliot described this by saying, "so little attention is paid to English at the preparatory schools that half of the time, labor and money which the University spends upon English must be devoted to the mere elements of the subject" (Eliot 1969, p. 100).

Because of a lack of secondary schools in the nineteenth century, some students came to college lacking the basic skills of spelling, writing, geography, and mathematics (Brier 1984). One of the strategies developed by universities to meet these needs was the formation of preparatory departments. These were designed to help students with the academic preparation they had not received earlier, and they proliferated on college campuses. "At many institutions preparatory enrollments matched or exceeded the 'regular' college enrollments" (Brubacher & Rudy 1976, p. 156). These programs were considered secondary schools within colleges and often led to a six-year program of study for underprepared students. One of the most enduring of the preparatory departments was created at the University of Wisconsin in 1849. It existed until 1880, despite being under continuous fire from the faculty (Casazza & Silverman 1996).

Widening The Crack in the Door

Beginning in 1862, the federal government became more directly involved in education at all levels. This involvement had a substantial impact on who would attend college, and it opened the doors to wider participation. One of the federal initiatives was the First Morrill Act signed by President Lincoln in 1862. This act guaranteed to each state 30,000 acres of land per congressman to support colleges dedicated to teaching agriculture and the mechanic arts. The Second Morrill Act, in 1890, further broadened the mission of universities by prohibiting federal funding to states that practiced discrimination in higher education.

The two Morrill Acts were significant in their combined effect on the evolving purpose of higher education. States began to establish A&M (agricultural and mechanical) universities and increased funding to public universities in order to provide more technical training. This funding was highly debated. Private institutions in the Northeast viewed government intervention as inequitable and quite threatening, to say nothing about whom it might bring into the halls of higher education. In addition to governmental calls for a change, business leaders were also demanding change; they wanted a curriculum that prepared students more directly for the job market. One Chicago businessman, Richard T. Crane, argued that "a college education, because of its classical and literary emphasis, was a worthless undertaking for any young man who wished to succeed in the business world" (Butts & Cremin 1953, p. 370).

In 1907, more than half of the admitted students to Harvard, Yale, Princeton, and Columbia did not meet the standard entrance requirements (Wyatt 1992). These schools then added developmental courses to their curricula. The most common of these were remedial reading and study skills courses. By 1909, over 350 colleges were offering "How to Study" courses for underprepared students, and by 1920, 100 study habit books had been published (Casazza & Silverman 1996, p. 20).

Also around the turn of the century, the concept of a junior college was growing. It began with four-year institutions creating two-year divisions within their overall university structures. The University of Chicago established a two-year liberal studies division, in order to create a natural break for students who were not able to go on for further study. Similarly, the University of Minnesota established its General College where 20 percent of its students had already failed elsewhere (Casazza & Silverman 1996). The General College was founded in 1932, with a general education curriculum that included introductory core courses and academic and personal counseling for students. It soon became well known for its curriculum and one of its early students, who could not pass the entrance exam for the Liberal Arts College, went on to win the Nobel Peace Prize in 1970 (Collins 2002).

The junior colleges within the larger universities were frequently used as terminal points for those not succeeding academically. Students were often counseled out after two years. Later in the 1970s, the growing community college system became another sorting point. Because of their policy of open admissions, they became a point of access for those denied admission elsewhere. They also provided an opportunity for those who had nontraditional goals: continuing education for self-improvement, vocational training, and transfer credit.

By 1917, seventy-six junior colleges had been established, which continued the trend of opening the doors of higher education to more students. The President's Commission on Higher Education stated the following: "Virtually 50 percent of the population has the ability to complete fourteen years of schooling, that is, through junior college and that nearly one-third has the ability to complete a college course in liberal arts or professional training" (Butts & Cremin 1953, p. 522). Within the next thirteen years, the number of college students doubled. This trend, of course, was hotly debated by educators who felt that there were already too many students enrolled who were below the more traditional standards. Nevertheless, higher education became more of an expectation for a high school graduate. In 1900, 1.6 percent of the college-aged population enrolled in college, and by 1960, it had increased to 22.2 percent (Cohen & Brawer 1982).

Even though more were attending college, students were increasingly segregated based on criteria such as goals, test scores, sex, and ethnicity. Admission requirements now included the new College Entrance Examination. This allowed colleges to quantify differences among students. Along with this, colleges and universities established separate schools to provide new curricula for science, agriculture, and engineering students. These courses of study were thought to be inferior by many in the liberal arts, and schools like Harvard created new degrees and certificates to accommodate the needs of the new and supposedly less capable students (Eliot 1969).

Despite the passage of equal opportunity legislation, which denied federal assistance to states if discrimination existed in their university admissions processes, the South continued to follow the policy of "separate but equal." New colleges, Tuskegee and Howard to name two, were founded to provide opportunities for Black students. These institutions were apt to provide instruction ordinarily considered to be below college level due to the lack of well-established, inclusive primary and secondary systems in the South. In their attempts to gain funding, these Black institutions were more successful if they sold themselves as trade schools rather than offering a traditional liberal arts curriculum. The legislatures were so adamant about this that at one Black institution, the only way to offer Latin was to call it Agricultural Latin (Brubacher & Rudy 1976).

Women, too, experienced their own discrimination, and they often attended colleges limited to female students. Many educators opposed college training for women and felt that their enrollment would lower the standards of universities in general. Some of the sentiments can be summed up in the following statement about women: "They were such delicate creatures, so different in mental as well as physical makeup from men, that they would never be able to survive the prolonged intellectual effort" (Brubacher & Rudy 1976, p. 65).

It is clear that students who had not had the opportunity for appropriate preparation in their high schools were being accepted to colleges and universities. Consequently, academic support systems began to grow. In 1929 a survey was sent to all state universities requesting information about their offerings in remedial reading. Almost 25 percent of those who responded indicated that they tried to identify poor readers upon admission, and slightly fewer actually provided some type of remediation (Parr 1930, p. 548). Some of the respondents had begun to implement mandatory remediation. At Ohio State University, probationary students were required to take remedial reading. One dean returned the survey with the comment, "I am sorry that we have nothing to report as done, but I am heartily delighted that you are beginning to work along this line. I don't know anything more timely" (Parr 1930, p. 548).

Book (1927) determined that in the fall of 1926 at Indiana University, only 27 percent of freshmen could find the main point of an assigned passage. He concluded that "the reading ability of college freshmen should be accurately determined; that special remedial instruction should be given to all who are found to be deficient in this regard; and that this instruction should be given in a special orientation or 'how to study' course and by an instructor who is specially interested in the work and well equipped to give the type of help which these students need" (p. 248).

Some colleges were giving credit to these remedial courses and at the same time hiring full-time staff to deliver the instruction (Barbe 1951). The courses were offered through a variety of organizational units, with a range of titles. When Harvard changed the name of its "Remedial Reading" course to "The Reading Course," enrollment increased from classes of thirty to classes that attracted hundreds of freshmen, upperclassmen, graduate students, and even professors from the law schools (Wyatt 1992).

Added to this increasing recognition that academic support systems were important was the unpredicted outcome of the Serviceman's Readjustment Act of 1944, more commonly referred to as the GI Bill. Originally written to reward military service following World War II and also to head off the potential economic chaos of so many G.I.s returning home from the war, this legislation had far-reaching effects. Under its education provisions, 2.2 million veterans were enabled to attend two- and four-year colleges and universities. Another 3.5 million enrolled in vocational schools. By 1947, veterans made up 49 percent of college enrollments (Greenburg 2004). Many of these returning veterans were married with children, and were often the first generation in their families to consider attending college. With this government funding, colleges developed guidance centers, reading and study skills programs, and tutoring services primarily to serve the new students (Maxwell 1979). Along with the veterans came increasing numbers of women, students with special needs, and students from impoverished backgrounds. Academic support systems grew and became more comprehensive to meet increasingly diverse needs.

MAKING ACCESS MEANINGFUL

Higher education had taken a new turn, and it is reflected in the charge of Gleazer (1970) to schools, "Meet the student where he is. I am increasingly impatient with people who ask whether a student is 'college material.' We are not building a college with the student. The question we ought to ask is whether the college is of sufficient student material. It is the student we are building, and it is the function of the college to facilitate that process" (p. 50). This was echoed by Cross, in 1971, who contended that, "Our initial reaction to that shock to our educational system was to organize remedial programs whose mission was to change the newcomers so that they would fit the requirements of traditional institutions. We did not, in the beginning, give comparable attention to changing institutions so that they would fit the needs of the new learners" (p. 10).

In 1973, the Carnegie Commission described an "educational revolu-
tion" in the 1960s when colleges began to offer "universal access." Its final
report reads, "The current transition to universal access to college involves
the guarantee of a place for every high school student who wishes to enter
higher education, the introduction of more remedial work, the adaptation
to the interests of new groups of students regardless of age...It is a
transformation of fundamental historic proportions" (Carnegie Foundation
for the Advancement of Teaching 1973, p. 5).

K. Patricia Cross described these "new" students in her classic text,
Beyond the Open Door (1971). Her research found that it was often the first-
generation college students who scored in the bottom third on traditional
tests of academic ability and viewed education as "the way to a better job
and a better life than that of their parents" (p. 18).

She also described them as ranking in the lowest third of their high
school class, as being passive toward learning, and bringing with them a fear
of failure. The failure syndrome was deeply embedded and was a result of
nonachievement at lower grade levels, leading to a heightened passivity
toward learning. This new student population was representative of a far
wider range of socioeconomic levels and ethnic and cultural backgrounds
than had ever enrolled in colleges and universities. Women and adults
comprised a large component of this group. From 1972 to 1982, the
number of adult students aged twenty-five to thirty-four attending college
increased by 70 percent and those over age thirty-five increased by 75
percent (King 1985).

Once again, federal legislation brought additional populations to the
doors of higher education. The Rehabilitation Act of 1973 made it easier
for students with disabilities to come through the doors, and it provided
assurances of academic assistance (Hardin 1988). Access for disabled students
continued to 1990 when the Americans with Disabilities Act was passed.
Schools were charged with providing "reasonable accommodation," and
with increased support at the elementary and secondary levels of the educational system, the number of students with disabilities entering college
continued to grow steadily. By 1994, 75 percent of adults with disabilities
had completed high school (U.S. Department of Education 1994), and
14,994 seniors took special editions of the Scholastic Aptitude Test (SAT).

Unfortunately, the doors that were gradually becoming more and more
open often turned into revolving doors as students began to regularly drop
out or stop out, the practice of enrolling in nonsequential terms. This led
to debates about how standards had been lowered and how they should be

raised in order to ensure that the doors opened only so far. The rapid growth of community colleges throughout the 1970s and 1980s led many to expect that underprepared students should be directed away from four-year institutions, and toward two-year schools. At several points, the General College at the University of Minnesota was considered for closing because community colleges were established in the Twin Cities (Taylor 2002). As Taylor notes, "Conflicted over the continuing presence of underprepared students in an elite research university...the President sought to improve the institution's financial status by adopting the University of Michigan model of higher admissions standards..." (p. 8). Although today the General College stands as a model for both practice and research related to underprepared students, it is once again being threatened with imminent closure by the Minnesota Board of Regents.

Community colleges have historically provided remedial education for their students. By 1965, over 60 percent of community college students ranked at or below the thirtieth percentile on the School and College Ability Test (Moore 1971). In addition, by the late 1960s remedial reading, writing, and math were the most frequently offered courses in community colleges (Roueche, Baker, & Roueche 1984).

In her classic text, Tomlinson (1989) articulates the debate over where developmental coursework belongs. If support were limited to community colleges, access to higher education would be denied to those potential students who live in areas where there are no community colleges. Those favoring assistance programs at all levels of postsecondary education argue that academic support needs to be specifically designed for each institution to ensure that its specific standards and expectations are met (p. 35). In other words, even if a community college did exist in a convenient location, its support system might not be appropriate for the four-year institution to which the student may transfer.

There are many examples of schools striving to combine access with excellence. In 1983, Robert McCabe, then president of Miami-Dade Community College, summed up one perspective by stating, "It is clear that standards have declined in American education at all levels....It is most important that we raise student expectations....The college should assume responsibility for assisting individuals to succeed, and an ordered curriculum should be instituted to deal with reading, writing, and computational deficiencies first, so that all students benefit from attendance" (p. 27). He urged colleges to hold their standards high, not by excluding students, but rather by testing all entering students and requiring them to take appropriate courses when the test scores indicated a particular academic need. He recommended early advising in order to help students understand how this would help them succeed. He also asked that schools develop flexible systems to allow reduced course loads for students needing additional assistance, and variable time frames for course completion. McCabe's recommendations were implemented at Miami-Dade Community College through mandated testing, placement into appropriate courses, and restricted enrollment. Students who participated in this were nine times as likely to graduate as those who did not participate (Roueche, Baker, & Roueche 1987).

McCabe's perspective was echoed by other educators. Cross believed that students needed assistance in order to overcome their fear of failure (Cross 1971), while John Roueche (1978) supported an intense program of academic assistance. He criticized what he believed to be a "Band-Aid" approach, enrolling students in a few remedial courses along with a full academic load. He recommended an integrated skills program for students to complete before taking core courses. By the Fall of 1989, 74 percent of colleges and universities offered at least one remedial course and 20 percent awarded credit for these courses (U.S. Department of Education 1991).

In addition to offering courses, another system for providing academic support began to grow in the 1970s. This was the learning assistance center. According to Arendale (2002), one of its distinguishing characteristics was that it delivered comprehensive services to all students, not simply to a subpopulation of underprepared students. The centers offered tutoring, workshops, counseling, and often faculty development for core faculty searching for practical advice on how to reach out to a wider range of students. They became a much more integrated part of the university mission. Faculty began to see the services as an extension of the classroom and as a means for developing more student mastery of the content they were teaching (Arendale 2002). Lissner (1990, pp.132–133) suggested that the centers were a natural evolution of programs that grew out of the Civil Rights legislation in the 1960s. Through those federal monies, a range of programs was created and it eventually became necessary to bring coherence to them, often through the centralization of a learning center.

Christ underscored how far this concept had developed from earlier, more isolated attempts to provide support when he said that learning assistance centers operated by "functioning as a campus-wide support system in a centralized operational facility; by vigorously opposing any stigma that it was remedial and only for inadequately prepared, provisionally admitted or probationary students . . . " (Christ 1997, pp. 1–2 as found in Arendale, p. 17).

Today a range of support systems exists successfully side by side. There is usually a positive synergy between the staff and the faculty who are responsible for the various components. For instance, the basic writing course may be delivered from an English Department or a more specialized Developmental Studies Department. The learning center may supply tutors to assist students inside or outside the classroom, and the tutors are often peer tutors recommended by content area faculty. The learning center may send a learning specialist into a classroom to deliver a workshop on time management to students. The learning specialist may also team up with a faculty member to integrate basic skills into a core course.

ACCESS AND SUPPORT TODAY

As the American population becomes more diverse and as high school students increasingly set their sights on a college education, postsecondary institutions must continue to evolve in order to meet the ever-changing demands. Access will continue to increase. Between 1960 and 2001, college enrollments increased from 4.1 million to 14.8 million. Ninety percent of high school seniors expect to attend college while only forty-seven percent of high school graduates have completed college preparatory curricula. Forty percent of students in four-year postsecondary institutions take remedial courses while the overall percentage for all institutions is fifty-three percent. Enrollment across colleges and universities is expected to grow, and by 2015, one to two million additional young adults will seek access, many of whom will come from low-income and minority families. In addition, the number of students over the age of twenty-five is projected to increase by 14 percent by 2010 (National Panel Report of the Association of American Colleges and Universities 2002).

At the same time, employers are looking for individuals who can process information and who possess good communication skills. A college education is no longer an option; indeed, it is becoming a requirement if one wants career choices. There are few unskilled jobs left today. As early as 1997, 96 percent of manufacturing firms indicated that they provided some education and training for their hourly employees. At least two-thirds of them also indicated that they provided remedial instruction in reading, writing, math, and problem solving (National Association of Manufacturers 1997 as reported by Roueche & Roueche, 1999, p. 2). From 1998 to

2008, 14.1 million new jobs will require a bachelor's degree or at least some postsecondary education, more than double those requiring high school or below (National Panel Report of the Association of American Colleges and Universities 2002).

Access to education is clearly a social imperative that must be taken seriously. Shaw (2002) reminds educators to broaden their theoretical base and to pay attention to the wider social framework and the role education plays "in providing students with the critical awareness and skills they will need to become active creators of social change, especially in responding to global issues" (p. 32). She urges educators to revisit the work of John Dewey and ask the following questions:

- What is the purpose of education in our society?
- How can education contribute to safeguarding and improving the best features of a democratic society?
- What sorts of educational approaches best prepare participants in our society to contribute most effectively to the common good? (p. 32).

These questions help to inform the debate which too often assumes that educational access is optional and that education is an entity separate from the rest of society.

Chapter 2

Belief in Students:
A Powerful Foundation ✨

> I guess my personal background has helped me in the field of developmental education because I know where these students are coming from and what they would like to accomplish. I hope that in some way I can serve as a role model to other developmental students and help them realize their dreams. (Santiago Silva)

INTRODUCTION

The voices recorded in this chapter describe in different ways the tremendous impact of believing in someone and of having a set of expectations for achievement. These two factors are prominent in the stories told here by educators and students across several decades. Martha Maxwell talks with admiration of her students in the 1950s and 1960s who today would be diagnosed as learning disabled, but who, back then, simply had to construct their own very time-consuming strategies in order to be successful. Calvin Mackie, currently a faculty member with a PhD who also took remedial reading in college, credits both his parents and a college teacher for believing in him and challenging him to set and meet high expectations. Several other students underscore the importance of being persistent and believing in themselves.

Many of the educators who have made a difference in the lives of underprepared students had early experiences that mirrored those of their students. Some came from immigrant families where education was an expectation, but there was no one to provide a model of exactly what that meant. Santiago Silva, formerly a vice president of a community college, was raised in a family of migrant farm workers with six siblings. His parents provided the encouragement for him to complete a formal education in order to break out of the migrant cycle. Likewise, Mike Rose, a widely published author and professor of Social Research Methodology at UCLA, grew up in a family that immigrated to Los Angeles in the early 1950s. He describes his high school days as "undistinguished" until he met a teacher who captured his attention and "awakened his brain."

One of the most interesting components of the stories told by these educators is the "two-way effect." They, in no way, feel like a savior or a depositor of skills into the heads of underprepared students. Instead, they are unanimous in the belief that they also gained much from the students. Robert McCabe, former president of Miami-Dade Community College, told us, "you will never forget what you will feel and what you get back from students that you really help." Juele Blankenberg, retired manager of tutoring services at a community college, was even more emphatic when speaking of this effect: "But those are gifts to me; I don't really know what gifts we give to students."

It is clear from their stories that these educators become involved with the students far beyond the classroom. They talk about the need to address the whole person and get past the notion of simply delivering instruction to a student. Individual students often have competing needs as they return to school while also managing their personal lives. In order to provide the most effective assistance, it is necessary to understand the complexity of the situation and to develop both the personal skills and the institutional systems that will help. This often includes challenging the system. David Taylor, former dean of the General College at the University of Minnesota, sums up his experience as an academic officer at the College of Charleston. He faced a vote of no confidence from the faculty when he made an exception for a student who was coming from a difficult family situation and needed to take extra credits. Likewise, Hunter R. Boylan, now director of the National Association for Developmental Education (NADE), describes how his evening conversations with the maintenance staff at his former university helped many of them realize their dreams as he worked with them to navigate the institutional system.

THE STORIES BEGIN

(We have kept the interview portions of the book informal, and, for the most part, have not adjusted the words to follow formal grammatical structure. Also in the interest of preserving a representative historical record, we have not altered either the language or contents of the stories to reflect our own views.)

◄₹ *Santiago Silva*

Santiago has been an officer in several professional associations related to working with underprepared students. He is currently a fellow in a national leadership program sponsored by the Hispanic Association for Colleges and Universities that is designed to prepare individuals for leadership positions in higher education.

I have a bachelor's degree in political science and history, an M.Ed. in counseling and guidance, and a PhD in counseling psychology. My test scores always indicated that I would not do well in a college setting. As a matter of fact, my high school counselor told me to go to a technical school and not waste my time in a "real" school. She indicated that I would never make it in college. I worked very hard as an undergraduate and as a graduate student because I always felt that I had to prove to my counselor that I could make it. I know that she did not tell me that I could not make it as a challenge; she really believed that I could not make it in a postsecondary setting.

I had parents who did not complete a formal education but were strong advocates of education. They always told me and my siblings that education would be the way for us to get out of the migrant farm work cycle. Although being a migrant farm worker taught me a great deal, I knew that I did not want to do that type of work the rest of my life. It was my parents' believing in me and my siblings and a great deal of hard work that got us all through our education. Among the seven children, we have four bachelor's degrees, three master's degrees, and two doctorates, not bad for former migrant farm workers.

I guess my personal background has helped me in the field of developmental education, because I know where these students are coming from and what they would like to accomplish. I hope that in some way I can serve as a role model to other developmental students and help them realize their dreams.

I did have several students who have had a significant impact on my career as a developmental educator. Two that come to mind are Sonia and Francisco. They were both students in the College Assistance

Migrant Program (CAMP) at the University of Texas-Pan American. They both came from humble beginnings, struggling financially, but determined to get an education. They both accepted the challenges before them and did excellent work. It was not easy for them, but they stuck it out and made it. What impressed me the most about them was their persistence and determination to make something of themselves. Not only did they excel in the classroom through hard work and dedication, but they were leaders among the rest of the students in their cohort. It was wonderful to see them mature and assert themselves not only in the classroom but in other university-sponsored events. Sonia went on to become an educator herself and is currently a 2nd grade teacher in Arlington, and Francisco is a pediatrician in Corpus Christi. I am so proud of them.

Quite honestly, I think that Sonia and Francesco would have succeeded without CAMP because they had the determination to make it. CAMP and its support services, however, provided the nurturing and support they needed, so they would not have to struggle as much to get the financial backing they needed. The program also provided them with a small stipend that helped them financially in addition to paying their tuition and fees. You need to remember that Sonia and Francisco, like so many of our Hispanic students or students of color for that matter, were first-generation college students. They had no role models before them. They were treading strange waters . . . the camaraderie that they developed while in CAMP helped them to assert themselves in a variety of settings including social and classroom. I would say it is the interaction between them and the program that helped many of the CAMP students. Not all of them were as strong personally and academically as Sonia and Francisco. You just knew that Sonia and Francisco were special the minute you met them. They served as role models for other students in the program and helped others excel.

Of course, there are numerous other success stories that I can share with you. It was seeing these students and so many others really work hard that confirmed for me that I was in the right profession. I had many opportunities, especially after I received my doctorate, to do other things, but it was seeing the faces of these students and how happy they were when they walked across the stage and received their degree that made me stay in higher education.

◄ᶾ *Nadege Meyer*

Nadege is a former graduate student whose primary goal is to teach under-prepared students at the college level.

I came from Haiti at the age of seven. When I came to the United States, I was placed in the 4th grade at a Catholic school. I had challenges with the class, so I was placed at a lower grade, at 3rd grade. From there, everything still wasn't going the right way. I wasn't able to pick up material or learn as fast as the other students. I came to the United States not knowing any English at all and was placed in a private school. I was never really tested to see why I wasn't able to do the work. I believe it wasn't until the 5th grade when my parents got me a tutor who spoke both French and Creole that she recommended that I should go to a public school where I was tested.

Until then I didn't really understand what was going on because at the time I was really soft-spoken. I just thought, hey, I couldn't do the work. My parents, I recall, they did speak with me about what was going on. It was hard for me to understand when they told me that they were considering me for special education. At the time, the kids at that age are really cruel, so they used words like "retarded" or "dumb." It was hard. It was hard being placed, going to another grade. And they even made it worse because the special education classes . . . there were children with special needs, but then again there were children that had not only learning disabilities but were in need of discipline also. It didn't add up at all, but I did stay there. I stayed in special education classes until my sophomore year in high school where I had a teacher that saw that I could do the work; it just took me a longer time to do the work. She spoke with my parents and spoke with the principal and decided that this wasn't the right place for me. So I was tested again. This test and the test that I took in the 5th grade were different. The test in the 5th grade, I think, it appeared to be more psychological just because the way the test was done. I was in a room; my father was there. There were about two or three psychologists. They just made, the way everything was done, made it feel like something was really wrong with me.

The teacher really pushed to get me out of the class, out of the special education classes, and started documenting everything that I was able to do the work. Yes, she worked closely with me but not as closely as with the others, and she suggested that my strongest point at that time was math. So she suggested that, let's not push her out there all at once, just every quarter, put her out for an extra class. So they put me out for math, and I was fine with that. Then they took me out for biology. That was fine. Then they put me out for English. I still see her, and she calls me her success. She was different from the others. She encouraged me with words. She just saw that I could do the work. Just seeing her . . . I would always come to her if I had any difficulty with classes. The door was always open for me to come to her. She was real with the whole class. Really, she understood. You know what I think; it was because her husband was of a different nationality also. So was the majority of the class with disabilities; they were from different nationalities. I think she was sympathetic toward that.

Going to college was always an expectation of my parents. My father finished 8th grade, but my mom did not. There were four of us, and we all went to college. It was just something that we had to do. My parents, even though they were told that I had challenges, they never really accepted that I could bring home Cs and Ds. They were never like that. They always looked for As and Bs.

There was an instructor in college my junior year that just stood out to me. It was a human resource class, and I took it one semester and had to drop it because I wasn't doing well in this class. So, I ended up dropping it. I tried taking it again, and I failed the class. The third time taking the class, I went from sitting in the back to sitting in the front, and he saw that I knew the material but when it came for the test I would just freeze. One day, he called me into his office and said to me, "Nadege, what's wrong? You know you're very involved in class; you answer questions. You do fine in class; you know the material. What's wrong?" I was like I just . . . I can't . . . I forget everything. So what he did was to allow me to take oral exams. I would do fine in the oral exams, but actually sitting there and doing it on paper, I just couldn't do it. I never approached him about my difficulties, but the fact that he picked that up . . . I was really, it really touched me.

◆? Mike Rose

Mike holds a PhD in educational psychology and is on the faculty of the UCLA Graduate School of Education and Information Studies. He has authored numerous articles and books, including Lives on the Boundary

(1989) and Possible Lives (1985), *which provide insights on the nontra-ditional student.*

O.K. Let's see. I went to elementary school and high school here in Los Angeles, to Catholic schools. I ended up going to Loyola University as an English major in 1962. I was admitted actually on a kind of provi-sional or probationary status because my high school record was pretty poor. It was only in my last year of high school that I was lucky enough to encounter an English teacher who kind of helped me catch fire. The final stage of my formal education emerged in the context of UCLA where I entered the graduate school of education as a doctoral student. I received my PhD in 1981.

I was one of those kids that so many of these programs are geared toward. My mother, father, and I migrated to Los Angeles in the early 1950s. They were very poor, and we lived in a fairly poor part of town. My education into high school, except for my last year, was pretty nondescript and uneventful and certainly undistinguished. You know, I was doing my usual drifting through high school thing; I was sleepwalking through school. But you know, like so many kids, I was just hungry for something, for anything. So we go into Senior English, and here's this guy who's maybe six or seven years older than us. He was sort of a beatnik kind of guy. His clothes were rumpled, and he tucked his tie between the buttons of his shirt rather than use a tie clip or anything. There was something about him that captivated me. He, first of all, demanded a huge amount of work. I mean here we were, all these kids, and he had us reading every-thing from the Iliad down through Hemingway. He expected papers every other week on these things, five hundred word essays. He worked; he worked his tail off for us. Somehow this just captured me. There was something about writing these essays; there was something about reading these books. I mean, I remember reading things like *Heart of Darkness* and not having a clue about what it all meant but really working at it.

The fact is that there was something he was doing that was making my brain come alive. All these different things drew me to him and, therefore, made me want to do well in his course. I really do credit him with getting me started, getting me oriented. He pushed me. He wouldn't take a second rate response, but he wouldn't have been breaking his back like that if he didn't think people could do it.

I'm sure in many ways my personal background plays into the kind of work I've done; the way I think about the work; and the way I understand the students who are the focus of the work. It operates on multiple levels, certainly on an emotional level and also a kind of existential level where there is some sort of joint participation in certain kinds of life work. And it absolutely operates on the level of cognition where I have always thought that we often misrepresent these folks, like me, and give us opportunities or curricula that are really way below what is possible for us. I certainly know what it is like to sit there and look at books and not know what you're reading.

I mean the way I see it is we are a composite of the people who taught us and the people we've read; people that I read all the way from Abraham Maslow and the kind of powerful sense that he gives of the possibility of human development to Martin Buber and the things he said about human relations. The use of those lenses to argue for, to demonstrate and argue for what people can do, even when it seems like they're blundering or taking missteps, is significant.

❧ Robert McCabe

Bob is a senior fellow with the League for Innovation in the Community College and a former president of Miami-Dade Community College.

I'm from Long Island and stopped out for part of my education years to work as a machine operator in an aircraft factory. I came back to school much more serious about it at the University of Miami. I got my master's at Appalachian State University and a PhD at the University of Texas in Austin. I certainly understand underprivileged students because I was one of them. In high school, I thought basketball was the world and the only thing that was important. I'm sure if anybody had any criteria other than "Could you play basketball?" when I went to Long Island University, then I would not have been admitted. I graduated when I was sixteen from high school, which was probably not a good idea. But after losing my basketball scholarship and going to work for a couple of years at a job that was just plain boring and had no future, the whole world looked different.

So that facilitated my understanding, particularly after having to drop out of school and spend a couple of years working as a milling machine operator, of what maturity means. I always say to people that maturity is great stuff. People are very often different after they're 22 or 23 than they are when they are 16 or 17, particularly if they've had some life experience. People are underprepared and not necessarily dumb, as people tend to characterize them. All of that certainly gave me an understanding of the importance of second chances.

One of the most important things in life is, first of all, to enjoy your work. Secondly, you must believe that you're doing something that is constructive and useful because what's really important is to be able to have a job where what you're doing makes a difference and particularly helps people who would otherwise not be helped. And it's important to get self-satisfaction out of doing that kind of work. The next thing I would say is to always remember that the job is about helping human beings to develop; it is not necessarily about gaining better skills in math. That is simply an instrument in helping people to grow. The last thing I will say is that you will never forget what you will feel and what you get back from students that you really help. If you're really there to help them, it will give you some life satisfactions that few people have.

❧ Thelma Coleman

Thelma returned to school twenty years following her high school graduation and persevered until she completed her BA in human services.

I didn't like high school that much. Well, I thought I didn't like it, but I found out later that it was only because I was sleepy. I am basically a night person. You know I guess my biological clock is kind of set differently from everybody else, and when I was in school I didn't sleep at night. You know everybody else would be asleep in the house and I'd be wide awake. Some nights I would go and sit on the front porch, and where I lived it was so quiet that I'd never see a soul walking down the street. I would just sit on the front porch late at night and watch the stars and think. By the time I'd go back in the house to go to bed, it was time to get up and go to school. So I used to be very sleepy, and I didn't understand then that I was fidgety in class and wanted to hurry up and get out of class. I used to think that I really didn't like school.

I wasn't always doing that well in math because for some reason it seemed like my math classes were always after my physical education classes. I liked swimming, so I would go swimming as many days as they would allow, so that meant I would always be late for math. When you miss things at the beginning of class, you get frustrated and don't do so well.

It was maybe twenty years or more before I went back to school after high school. It was a very, very long time. I think even after I got married I thought about how I should go back to school. By the time I made up my mind, I discovered we were getting ready to start a family and school got put on the back burner and stayed there for a long time.

The most influential person for my learning was a counselor that I once had. I met her after I was an adult, and I had been telling her that I was going back to school to take some courses. I was working nights, midnights as a matter of fact. She asked me why I was always talking about going back and why I had not done it because my children were not kids anymore, so it wasn't that I had to worry about having a babysitter and everything. So I thought about it, and I said "well I guess she had a point there." So one day I went out to the next registration day for one of the junior colleges, and I signed up to take some courses; it seemed as though that was the coldest day of the year. There weren't any teachers there. There was a person in the registrar's office who said that I must really want to start school because I came when it was so cold and nobody else was there. She was the person who got me started, and I kind of became what I call a drop in student for quite a number of years because I had to keep stopping my education. First it was because of money, and I couldn't get financial aid. When I ran out of money, I had to stop. A couple of my instructors had told me though that I had lots of perseverance, and I never thought of myself that way until I realized that I never gave up the things I wanted to do.

And after that took awhile, I said "well I think I need more than a certificate now." Maybe I should try to get my associate's degree, but then I ran out of money and I had to stop. Then I also lost my job, so I started back to school under the Dislocated Workers Program in the city, which paid for my tuition and books and even reimbursement for carfare. I got my associate's degree, and I was told about, well, I was thinking about getting a degree in social work, but a lot of universities that I was thinking about going to didn't want to accept for credit a lot of the courses that I had already taken. And considering that I was not seventeen or eighteen years old and just graduating from high school, I did not want to go and take all of those courses all over again you know.

I had only a couple of bad experiences that were kind of minor. One was a comment made by a teacher once when I mentioned about going on to get a degree in psychology. He was very negative about it and said that only people just getting out of high school should even consider going on to get a degree. For a moment I just listened to him, but you know, instead of feeling bad about what he said, I just figured he was kind of a jerk. So I just ignored him because had I listened to him, I would have been ready to just say, "well I guess there is no need for me to go on because I am not a teenager anymore." Most of my teachers were very encouraging, and I know that I had this biology teacher who once gave us a test. I got a 98 on it, and he called me in and asked if I was all right because I had only gotten a 98. Well you know it made me feel good that he had these high expectations of me because he said I always did well and got good grades.

❧ Dawn Harrington

Dawn received a BA in English at National-Louis University and would like to work in the field of journalism as an editor.

Well, first I come from a single parent home, and I would definitely say that my mom influenced my learning the most. She gave me a push in education, and she is my role model. She started college maybe twenty years ago but never got a chance to finish because of financial responsibilities, so I went on because of her. I wanted to be a teacher because I loved my English teacher in high school, Mrs. Burnburg. I still remember her. She was so excited when I told her I wanted to be an English teacher. She was so proud that I think tears came to her eyes as soon as I told her.

I think in grade school and high school I was let down by the educational system. I think I was really let down. Thinking back on the classes I had; I had a math class for the last two years of high school where kids were throwing spitballs. I don't think I even learned any math, and now I am definitely not doing math. Kids were treating teachers like they were a joke, and school just became a waste of time. Back to my mom though, during this time she pushed me to go ahead and try to make the situation work for me, work in my favor. As far as math and science, those classes were a big joke, and I think that is why I am lacking those skills right now. I am a history and English major.

◄ Hunter R. Boylan

Hunter is the director of the National Center for Developmental Education at Appalachian State University. He has been the lead researcher in nationally recognized studies related to best practice for underprepared students. His latest book is What Works: Research-Based Best Practices in Developmental Education.

I grew up in what you'd call a lower-middle-class household. Before I'd gotten out of Steubenville, Ohio, and learned more about the world, I thought I was poor. In retrospect, I didn't realize what poor was.

I played football, was captain of the tennis team, and president of the student council, yet there was always this class separation between me and some members of the "in crowd." I began to understand class differences quickly as I was growing up. When I was in college at Miami University of Ohio, a fairly ritzy school as it seemed to me then, it seemed as if everybody had lots more money than I did and a condescending attitude toward people who were poorer than they were.

I began to understand this concept of looking down on people from the wrong end. I became a real defender of the underdog. My own experience suggested that being an underdog doesn't necessarily mean you can't do what you want to do. I said, "Okay, I'm able to overcome this." And to be honest, it wasn't that damned much to overcome. I mean, I was a White male. I had a good education. I got good grades. It just felt like I was the underdog. And I suppose young people will do that. They magnify all the circumstances in their environment and aren't able to look at it in perspective. But I did develop an attitude: "I'm going to overcome whatever I see as a challenge, and I'm also going to help other people."

Skipping forward, through a variety of circumstances, I wound up working with street gangs in north Philadelphia. This was in the late 1960s. The street gangs in north Philadelphia were primarily African American or Puerto Rican. I also worked at Temple University as an assistant dean of men there. The salary was so bad; I moonlighted as a gang control worker. During the day I'd work with college students who seemed to be something of a disorganized rabble. They couldn't get their act together to do much, and they didn't do much in the way of organized social events. They didn't do much in the way of intellectual events. They sort of waited for somebody to hand it to them. If somebody put together a concert in the concert hall, they'd go.

Meanwhile, the street gangs were out there with no resources whatsoever. They were always having activities, organizing things, were pretty highly motivated, and they communicated well. And they were very effective at what they were doing. In fact, they were much more effective at being street gang members than college students were at being college students. And so I thought, "You know, these guys have all the characteristics they need for success except for the opportunity to attend college." I began trying to encourage some of them to attend Temple University. I got a couple of them into the Upward Bound Program and then worked with them myself, just sort of individually once they got to Temple University, to help them succeed. I think that's where my developmental education started.

See, the War Lord of the Omega Soul Gents was one of my students. I thought we were doing really well with him. The guy managed to make the transition from the streets to campus and even got reasonably good grades. At least he had a 2.2 or 2.4 grade point average after his first semester. After his second semester, he came back to my office and said, "Hunter, I'm leaving because college is something you have to make a commitment to, and you got to spend time at it. And every minute I spend on campus studying and doing college things or something, it takes me away from the street. I can feel my street skills atrophying, and I can't afford to do this. I'm just going to have to quit and go back to what I know."

And I realized in talking to him, and it took me awhile to figure this out, that we had failed him. We didn't realize what was going on in his life. We were very happily tutoring him in English and talking to him about how to register and giving him academic advising, but we never paid attention to the fact that it's a horrible transition to go from living on the streets, which he literally did. Now you know why I realized I wasn't really poor when I was growing up. I didn't realize the transition it was to be a college student coming from that background.

Basically, he said, "Look, you can flunk out of college, and you're still alive. You screw up in the street, and you're dead." He had a great influence on me in terms of helping me to recognize what we were missing in dealing with students. Their lives had more to do with their success in college than my petty tutoring support.

I met him ten to fifteen years later. I was giving a speech in Pennsylvania for TRIO (federal grant program) personnel. This guy comes up to me afterward and shakes my hand thanking me for everything I did for him. I told him I was sorry but I didn't recognize him and he said, "Well, that's because you knew me better as Bubby Tomatoes." It turned out he had gone on to a community college later. Actually he transferred to a university and got a graduate degree and was working in a Talent Search program. Guess what they do in Talent Search? They go out and find talented disadvantaged young people who might have potential for college. So he had dropped out for a while. He was probably a twenty-five-year-old college graduate.

I was working at a university in Ohio, and Linda was a maintenance worker in our building. She was an African American woman about nineteen years old with two children. I worked late, and she would always come in and clean the office and empty trash cans while we talked. She'd talk about how much she wanted to go to college, how she just enjoyed being on a college campus and wished she could become a student. So I said, "Well, gee, if that's what you want, let's work it out." By that time, I was pretty good at working with disadvantaged students. I got her a scholarship, but there were some problems. She had a GED (high school equivalency degree) in another state, but that state's standards weren't as high as Ohio's. I had to go a few rounds with the admissions' and registrar's offices. When the dust settled, we got her in. We got her a scholarship and she, too, turned out to be a solid student. She got a couple of Bs, a couple of Ds and a couple of Cs, but she was moving in the right direction.

Then she began having dental problems. The kind of stuff you get when you have never had dental care. She, too, was awfully poor. I went all over trying to find a way to get some free dental care for her, but there wasn't any available. I couldn't find anything, and I was pretty resourceful.

Eventually, she came in and thanked me for everything I had done but said she was leaving school. She had to go back to work in order to make enough money to get her dental problems taken care of. She was in so much pain that she couldn't study. What I didn't realize was that going to work meant going to Detroit and becoming a hooker. I later heard that she was killed in that duty. We lost her because we couldn't get $500 worth of dental work done. She wound up hooking on the streets of Detroit, and somebody beat her to death. I'm not sure what I learned from that except to be angry and to recognize, once again, how life affects students' success.

A lot of the students I worked with were from various ghettos. We recruited them off the streets of Detroit, Cleveland, and Toledo. When I first came to work at this university, they looked at my résumé and said, "Gee, you've worked with street gangs, so that means you can work with our Black students." And so whenever some problem came up with Black students, I got dragged into helping solve it. But then again, it turned out that I was the White administrator that they had the most positive dealings with. I wound up becoming one of their advocates and even the advisor to both the Black and Latino student unions, which they told me was not bad for a White boy.

I was an officer in the military. You learn things there about working with people, about leading personnel. My leadership training came in very handy. When a student came into my office, his problem got solved. I wasn't afraid to break eggs to make the old omelet. My guess is that my actions over time caused students to trust me . . . they learned they could depend on me.

It's imperative to recognize that college is what takes place while life is going on. What happens in life is vastly more important to one's success in college than what you're doing in college. That's hard to swallow. You want to believe that you make all the difference. I've learned that, compared to what's going on in someone's life, you make relatively little difference. You might make a 5 percent or 10 percent difference; for the majority of the people I've worked with, that percentage is enough. Part of it is understanding how their life connects to their circumstances and how that connects to their academic performance.

❧ Lola Romero

Lola received her GED after being out of school for thirty-seven years and currently works in the Radiology Department at a university medical center. She is also enrolled in a BA program, and she is working toward a degree in radiology.

My great grandmother had the most influence on me as far as an education goes. The things she told me as a child have never been forgotten, and I even tried to pass the stories on to my own four children. She was my whole world as she raised me until I was nine years old. My mother gave me up when I was born in order to finish her own education and then married and moved away, so I knew no other family besides my two grandmothers. My one grandmother continued to pay for my private schooling until her death. I was able to finish 9th grade in a Catholic school, and I feel that put me on the level of a senior in a public high school then. I was a straight A student then, and I think that accounts for me passing the GED test thirty-seven years later.

We were in the lunchroom at work one day, and the supervisor asked me where I went to high school. I said that I didn't go to high school, and she wondered how I had gotten into my job without a high school background. So I thought: I need a high school diploma quick. I called the adult school to see how I could get a GED, and they told me all I had to do was to bring in my birth certificate and take a test. That all took time, and meanwhile the supervisor kept asking me how I got hired without a diploma. I kept fluffing her off and making jokes, but I finally went to the adult high school and told the lady I wanted to take a GED test. She told me I had to take classes, but I didn't have time to take those classes. She warned me that it would be throwing away my money if I paid for the test with no preparation, but I insisted and I went and took the test and passed. I don't know how I passed.

I remember when I was five years old going to the bank with my grandma and watching her sign papers with an "X," and the man at the bank signing along with her. I asked her in the car how come she didn't sign her name like he did, and she told me that she didn't know how to read or write. She told me then that she would pay for my schooling as long as she could so that I would be smart enough to do her business and sign her papers. I remember how that made me feel, and that same feeling was inside me the day I registered for college. And the day I get my degree, I know my grandma will be right there cheering me on.

The day I was ready to drop out of my biology class, I do believe she was there to help me find the support I needed. Since I never went to high school, I never had a class in biology. Well, the instructor returned our tests one day, and I found that I had failed the test. Right then I had to get to a place in my mind where I didn't walk out of class. So right then I had to like think of things real fast; okay these are the things that went right through my mind then: I'm fifty-five years old. I've been out of school for forty years, and some of these other girls have been out of school for like a year. I never went to high school; I never had a biology class. These girls just had biology last year, and we all failed the test but I failed with the highest number of points. I had to put myself in a spot where I had confidence right then. I felt a responsibility to myself. I did not want to walk out of that class. I needed to put my mind in a frame where I could sit there with an "F" grade. I was totally devastated, totally. I needed to put myself in a frame where I could sit there because I wanted to run.

I try harder than the average student because I don't want anyone to have anything negative to say about my age playing a part in this. The most challenging part for me is my own insecurities; I find them a daily battle, but I am stubborn and do not accept "no" gracefully. In fact if someone says, "Lola, I don't think this suits you," it's on! I can do anything I put my mind to. I have always been willing to learn.

When I first went to college, I took placement tests and the math test determines which math classes you have to take and the English test determines what English classes you have to take. When I first took the test, I went to see my counselor, and the results indicated that I should start with basic math. He told me to take the test over again. I refused, but he told me that I must have been tired when I took them. He believed that I could do better since I had been a bookkeeper for fifteen years. Well, I went and studied for the math test and took the test again. I knew that I probably did not pass it, but I did.

You know when I'm in some classes I don't feel like I'm an older student at all. I blend right in. I don't know; I thought it would bother me. The first day of school, I started to not go, but my husband told me to go. I was afraid, and I told him that I was too old and that I just should not be there. When I got there I wasn't the oldest student in class. There were actually two men older than me; the guy who sat right next to me was my age.

David V. Taylor

David is the former dean of the General College at the University of Min-nesota. While there, he promoted new initiatives and helped to develop a

nationally recognized research base for the college. David was active pro-
fessionally in the community surrounding the university and has led several
research projects investigating ways to support disadvantaged youth. He is
currently the vice president of Academic Affairs at Morehouse University.

I am still impressed thinking about the only African American teacher I
had during my early educational experience. He was my 7th grade
mathematics teacher, and I was only one of four African Americans in an
accelerated math curriculum. This teacher nurtured us and taught us
how to appreciate mathematics.

In high school, I was one of the few Black students in the advanced
math/science courses, but somehow, they had in their mind, the
thought that I couldn't do it. My teachers thought that college work
would be too difficult for me, and they encouraged me not to go to the
university. I went on to the University of Minnesota, and there, again, I
found myself in the minority, being in the College of Liberal Arts with
only a few Black students, freshmen that made it into the college and
not into the education program. I was one of four African American
students from St. Paul Central High School admitted that year. The
other three were admitted to the General College. I was told by my
high school guidance counselor that even though I appeared capable,
the University of Minnesota would be too great a challenge for me.

I thought that was kind of interesting. And so, my whole career went
that way. For graduate school in history, I was still the only Black
student doing that sort of part and certainly at the PhD level. So I was
always kind of curious as to why I was able to succeed and have support
and others didn't, and the mixed messages that I was giving them. So, I
thought that if I could get into higher education and do my thing on the
side, I might be able to work with other students who had experienced
similar dissonance in their developmental background.

Very seldom did I have anyone to talk with me about career as-
pirations. So, having access to students who are nontraditional, I've
become a role model because I have worked through all the politics and
all of the hurdles to get to where I am. Another source of satisfaction for
me is probably the programmatic success I've had here at the General
College, a program designed for nontraditional students and students
from a wide variety of backgrounds who catch the interventions that we
present to make them more successful. Certainly, my work as a historian
has brought me satisfaction also because what I've done is gone back to

research the history of the community that was responsible for my success. I've been able to publish and turn those stories back over to the community to inspire other students about what is accomplishable given the backgrounds that they've had.

I recall at the College of Charleston, South Carolina, I came in as the first Black academic officer the school had had in its twenty-year history. And my first test case, which almost brought me a vote of no confidence by the faculty, was the case of a White student, who was brilliant, coming out of a difficult family situation, which might have been an abusive situation. She wanted to get out of school in a hurry, get out of her family, but that would have required her to take twenty-four credit hours, and we were on the semester system. She had a particular genius for languages and wanted to go off into international business using her language background, but she really wanted to get out of school. I talked with her, and we decided that I was going to make an exception, allow her to register for 24 credit hours. The faculty thought I was crazy and that if this was an indication of my leadership, then maybe I wasn't a match for the college.

She persevered, she finished the semester with a 3.2. All she needed was someone to believe that she could do it and to give her the encouragement and the emotional support; I was there. Of course, they didn't applaud me for it; I mean that kind of insight, judgment, but I'll bet she's doing great and wonderful things now.

On the other hand, when I was working at the State University of New York, I had a lot of students coming out of New York City whose goal was to get a degree; they didn't care what they got the degree in, and they didn't care how they got the degree. All they knew was that a degree was a passport to a better life. And so, I had to work with them and the faculty to address them, as it were, and tell them that it was not a degree factory. Their intrinsic value should be in learning the content that goes into the degree; that should be the focus and then other things will follow from that. And so working with a value system that way, I was attempting to correct the value of higher education for a nobler end.

I think we need to be receptive to ability and potential however we find it and however we can engage that and invite it into the academy. We must create academies that are warm and nurturing and supportive learning communities that don't have biases that tend to exclude. Rather we must be supportive of anyone who is willing to work hard and take the opportunities that are there. But when we get to the point where we become more exclusionary, especially in an era where more students are not being prepared for the rigors of higher education, it's kind of self-defeating.

✑ Gladys Shaw

Gladys is the retired program director for Student Support Services at the University of Texas at El Paso. She has been very involved at the national level in setting standards of practice for academic support services in colleges and universities.

I have a master's degree in education and business and am also a CPA and CSP. I was a first-generation, low-income student before we recognized them as such. I got married in high school and, even though I was the class valedictorian, I was denied a scholarship because I was married. So at that point, I was a little desperate. I wasn't sure how I was going to go to college, but we made it. We worked; we dropped out; we worked, and we went back and finally graduated in 1955 after starting in 1947. I loved to go to school from the first day I went, and I loved to read.

My dad was a reader. He wasn't an educated man, but he was a reader, I think he was my main influence. He never directly told me I had to go to college, but he set a good example for me. I wanted to be a doctor, I thought. I had worked in a hospital, a little clinic, when I was about fifteen. That sort of challenged me, and I liked that, but my husband's father was a doctor and he was pressuring him to be a doctor. So he went into premed, and it kind of occurred to us, since there wasn't any financial aid, we couldn't both go into medical school at the same time.

I switched to business and education. I'm glad I did; that was far better for me. It's just where my heart is; it's where my passion is. Education has made such a difference in my life that it just, you know, I could just see that I could make a difference there. I went in as a provisional student because I came from an unaccredited high school. Then they tested me, and I placed out of a lot of stuff. It was a very small college, about eight hundred students, and some of the instructors took a real interest in me. I got scholarships and things, so that really, really helped a lot and I think really influenced me.

I had two business instructors who were just wonderful, and I had, well he was the dean of the College of Business. The dean of the college kept his eye on me. You know, the academic dean, and it was a very supportive environment. I didn't even know I was getting scholarships, and they just went through. I didn't even know there was a possibility of work, but someone let me know, and I worked for the head of the department the whole time I was in college. Every professor knew every student, and every student knew every professor on campus. It was a total learning community; really, that is what it was.

I have tried to practice the same way as an educator myself, and there are many students who have had an impact on me. I think, in general though, the ones who really, really spur me on and motivate me are the ones who are working against the odds and are trying really hard. I think of one example of a young woman I had in my class who had three small children and her husband was disabled, totally disabled, and she was trying to come to school. And her husband was not a nice person. You know, she was sort of stuck with him, and of course she loved her children and wanted to do better for them. And she really had a lot of adversity and was persevering. And, you know, I look at that and I look at my life and I think, "Man, I've got it easy." And education is what made the difference of course.

I've stayed in touch with some of my students. In fact, one of them was working as a maid, and she didn't speak English. She started in my class and she has just finished her degree in physical therapy. Yeah, I'm in touch with her; in fact, her sister cleans my house. You know her sister doesn't speak English, and she hasn't gone to school like Rosa did. Rosa, it took her about six or seven years, but she's there now. We see them every day here; you know we really do. You see these returning, single parents and these guys who are trying; I don't see as many guys trying as hard as women though. There aren't as many guys coming to college for one thing. It may be an ego thing; I can't assess it. I just know they don't fall into the study routine, and they're not willing to put in the time. But the young women are. The guys are less willing to ask for help, and when you go to try to help them they don't always access it.

And sometimes I see them (guys) clowning. I know that's not what they want to be, you know, clowning around. And sometimes it's difficult to reach students like that. I had one young man who was so frustrated, and he told me that. And I thought, "OK." But he just couldn't do a single assignment even though he wanted to learn. You know you just can't do it that way.

I get closer to the women in the class as a rule. Now I've had several male students who have become really good friends, but as a rule I think it's easier to communicate and connect with the women. They will stay after class. For example, I had one older lady. She was in her fifties or sixties last semester. Our class was at 7:00 P.M., so I would go down at 6:15 P.M. And she would come early, so we could practice on her English, you know, before class. But I couldn't see a guy doing that.

◄◄ Dana Britt Lundell

Dana directs the Center for Research on Developmental Education and Urban Literacy (CRDEUL) at the General College of the University of Minnesota. She is the author of numerous articles and co-edits the CRDEUL *monograph series.*

I saw a disconnect between my own personal experience in school and that one my parents were talking about. The disconnect was probably caused by the location where I grew up; it was a higher socioeconomic class and a very homogeneous, White student environment. But I actually visited my mom's school a lot in the Dayton public school system, and I kind of lived every day with stories and conversations, and I got to know her students and a lot of the teachers in the Dayton public school district. That was just a big contrast in terms of, you know, a lot more students of color and I was very aware, I think, of the class issues on some level growing up.

I didn't know what I expected as a tutor. I just sort of immersed myself in it probably because I just enjoyed writing. I really like the tutoring process and was very drawn to the level of engagement that you have as a tutor in terms of just working side by side with people. Actually I just remembered one other experience. I think it was like in 4th or 6th grade. I remember they teamed, it was like a peer tutoring thing they had set up. It was within our own school system. We would sit in the lunchroom and they had a thing that they experimented with for a while that was a form of peer tutoring. They didn't do this very long term. I think it was my earliest actual tutoring experience. So I think I was always drawn to that sort of interaction.

Students who I would consider the returning adult students, or returning students, are the ones who have had the greatest impact on me.

Anywhere from students who maybe returned, say, they've worked awhile and they come back at maybe age twenty-four. They've been out three, four or five years working, and they return to college. I think a lot of these students stand out in my mind because they bring such incredible experiences with them. They really know why they are in college. It's really a choice and they are very overt about why they've come back. They can articulate connections both to their jobs, you know, their working situations and why education is important. And also, they will articulate it more on a level of personal development and other values they've formed in terms of what they see as privilege in terms of being able to get an education.

I think students in my writing classes, writing about their educational and literacy experiences, have made an impact on me. These particular students, I could just picture several of them in my mind. I found them to be very engaged students. They just brought a lot to the classroom. They have made me reflect on the purpose of education. They were able to articulate things for me. They have educated me . . . a lot.

Jane Neuburger

Jane is the director of the Learning Resource Center at Syracuse University. She currently chairs the National Certification Council for the National Association for Developmental Education.

My first year of teaching was in the southeast Bronx in New York City. My responsibility was to teach English to 9th graders. This meant writing and literature; I went into a situation where I had no books to give to the students. The students came in with no papers, no pencils. I had no classroom of my own because I was a new teacher, so I had a different classroom for every class period. There was a policy of social promotion, which meant that if you were a student, you could only be held back once in kindergarten through 6th grade and once again from 7th grade through 12th grade.

What I found was that once students got behind, they stayed behind. My homeroom was 9V; those were in the days when we grouped students homogeneously, and they were a really troubled group. I discovered that they couldn't read, certainly not at the 9th-grade level or even at the 8th-grade level. The best I could expect was the 6th-grade level, and there was a large contingency who was reading somewhere between the 3rd- and 4th-grade level which is just about the difference between sight vocabulary and phonics. So these students didn't know their phonics well. That coupled with social promotion, I felt, was doing these students a terrible, terrible disservice. Education is supposed to be the great equalizer, yet we sometimes provide no books, no homework expectations, and no consequences. Those children then, when they actually got out of high school (because I won't say they graduated), I think they had a right to be angry. We really have submitted them, or confined them, to a life of poverty if they were reading at that sort of level.

That influenced my decision to pursue my master's degree in reading because I certainly wasn't able to teach English. My second year of teaching, I wound up working on Staten Island, another borough of New York City, in a reading lab. It was a federally funded program, and I did have books and materials. You could work really hard with the students and help them work on strengthening their skills. They came in with paper, pens, and pencils from home. I think the socioeconomic background was a little bit higher. I could really see the students were progressing, not only on the reading comprehension test, but also reading at a deeper level of comprehension. So that experience influenced my eventually becoming a developmental educator. On the one hand, I had a real experience where I could see the seriously disadvantaging issues that some students were facing in high school prior to ever even thinking about going to college; and on the other hand, I worked with a group of students in need of additional reading work and was able to make a difference.

There was a student in the southeast Bronx who used to whore in the back hallways for bubble gum. There was a student, a first-generation Hispanic young man, whose parents made him work in his uncle's store after school to keep him out of trouble; the store was robbed, and the young man took off after the robber. And on his way back, his uncle mistook him for the robber returning and shot him. He died. Then there was a student whose younger brother was playing leapfrog from building top to building top on Mother's Day and fell to his death. And there was a student (this is the same student who was whoring for bubble gum) whose brother was playing Russian Roulette with his friends and lost. He shot himself to death.

As far as I know, these problems were not addressed in the classroom. Whether or not counselors were available, I just don't know. There was one student who had been on my roster as absent the entire previous year, 284 days. I began to wonder, based on these other experiences, if he was even alive, so I talked to the students and they said, "Oh no, Miss. He comes in every day for breakfast and for lunch." So I told them to have him come and visit me. He did. He filled the doorway at 6'5" and about 200 pounds. I think I can understand why this huge boy was not comfortable in a 9th-grade setting. Anyway I marked him present for the day so that the next year people wouldn't have the same question about whether or not he was alive. Think, for a moment, how telling that statement is.

Looking back now, I realize that I was not prepared to *teach* in such a survival zone, but my heart knew that education was the way up and out of the nightmare my students were living. Many developmental students face significant challenges in their lives, and these stories serve to remind us of our great responsibilities. I don't know if any of my 9th graders ever made it out of the Bronx, but I remember the challenges they faced each day to simply make it to school and home alive, and I remember that when I'm in front of a class of developmental students or when I'm advising, or when I'm assigning a tutor. I certainly don't know all of the struggles my current students have overcome in order to be sitting in front of me, but I sure know that I will do all I can to help them succeed from this point on.

I started, as I think many of us do, as a classroom teacher, and very, very involved with my students and their success. And I hope never to lose that. I think that it's important for anyone who works with students or helping others. That all of it stems from one-on-one success or in the classroom. You know, you count your evaluations, one student at a time. You really do. So, those success stories are really, really important. It's really important to work with your deans, with your college presidents. Understand where they are coming from whether you agree or not . . . we need to be adamantly steadfast that *our* students are *their* students as well. They need to hear individual student stories and numbers. Send out those success stories in memos, newsletters, and brag about your students. After all it's always been about the students. If we can focus on student success as our common goal, we can move mountains. We can change the world, one student at a time.

◄? Juele Blankenberg

Juele, now retired, was the manager of Tutoring Services at Oakton Community College in Illinois. She frequently taught graduate courses in the field of developmental studies.

I went through the civil rights movement, and it became really apparent to me that marching in the streets wasn't really productive and that education was more useful, so I became a Human Relations trainer. Out of that came my interest in developmental education because at that point I realized that a lot of folks who needed a great deal of help were really needy in very clear basic skills.

I'm one of the believers that developmental education means that I'm here to try to facilitate your moving from where you are to where you want to be. I think that can happen at any level of education, not just basic skills. We see evidence of that need all around. Certainly medical schools, graduate schools, all kinds of institutions are beginning to understand that the desire to achieve your own goal, to achieve your own excellence, is important.

What do I contribute to students? Now, this sounds almost mundane, but it begins with the fact that I really like them and that they feel safe with me. I think that I make some kind of contribution to the environment. One other thing that's interesting is that I still get to tutor. I tutor all kinds of odd things, and that's really a gift from the student to me. Like I have just gone through Socrates' *Myth of the Cave*, which I would not have had a chance to look at again if it hadn't been for the student who couldn't understand it. So, I had to refresh and get on with all that. But those are gifts to me; I don't really know what gifts we give to the students.

◄? Nancy Bornstein

Nancy is the director of the Learning Center at Alverno College, a liberal arts college for women nationally known for its innovative competency-based curriculum and system of assessment. She served as the president of the National College Learning Center Association and was coeditor of The Learning Assistance Review.

I was hired to teach this high school equivalency (GED) class, and I absolutely loved working with adults who were trying to catch up, in a sense, to learn things they hadn't learned. I taught myself what the GED was and what was entailed in teaching that coursework. From there, I decided that was more my calling than political science or teaching elementary school. At that time there really wasn't any graduate preparation for teaching in any of the fields that related to that population whether it was Adult Basic Education, GED studies, or developmental education. People came to it from different disciplines and areas of interest, somehow connected to it and fell in love with it; this is what I've always seen as one of the really good things about this field.

The first GED class I had was a group of women who were, for the most part, in their thirties and forties and wanted to get their high school equivalency. We had class in a basement. When I say basement, it was in a basement, in a housing development apartment of one of the women in the class. The women who lived there wanted this opportunity. They sought out this class and brought it home so they were able to attend. It turned me on so much to see that, and I think that really formed how I see working with students.

Just that opportunity to connect to somebody and figure out what education meant to them and how they really felt it could give them access and freedom they never had before. I've always believed this experience shifted my view of education; that's why I think working in this field is so critical. Being able to release the promise they have is really pretty incredible. I think we do that most every day in this field.

There have been a few students in particular that I just bonded with. I don't know who got more out of that experience. You know, being able to work with someone and feel like you were not just their teacher; their successes were my successes.

◄᠍ Gail Platt

Gail is the director of the Learning Center at South Plains College in Texas and has been actively involved nationally and particularly across the state of Texas in professional organizations.

I was always very attracted to language, language arts as an English major. I always felt comfortable with the written and spoken word, yet I always found it a challenge to perform in math. I avoided math; I was not interested in math. In high school I sat in the back of the room, read magazines, wrote notes and letters, and did everything but pay attention to what the teacher was trying to teach. When I got to college, I found out that I was very well prepared for the language arts components, all those liberal arts classes but not well prepared for the math and science components. So I had tutors and took advantage of support services that would help in the math area. I found that a lot of it was attitudinal; I didn't think that math was very important, and since I didn't think it was important, I hadn't paid attention. I needed to develop those aspects cognitively and know that it was possible to do that. If we look at the research in the area of cognitive development, there is certainly evidence there to suggest that adults do continue to make dramatic gains throughout adult years.

I think this is the situation for many college students, that we are interested in certain things; we like certain things; we find certain things rewarding to us and so we concentrate on those areas. There are certain areas we don't enjoy and we don't find rewarding, so we neglect them. I think it is really important to consider that for every student at every college and university there is something that academic support services or developmental education can offer. Again, I made straight As in English, but math was not my forte, so I needed help in math. Most of our students are not outstanding in every area, so while they may have very strong skills in many areas, there may be one academic discipline where they do need assistance.

David Arendale

David is a former president of the National Association for Developmental Education and currently an associate professor at the General College in the University of Minnesota. His major discipline is history, and he has written numerous articles on access in the context of the history of higher education.

I have been impacted particularly by the middle-aged students I taught at several community colleges. I suppose it was because they were so diverse in terms of the student population, and back in the 1980s that was a really high time period for the returning adult student. So, as I think about my experiences with these students, it's probably seeing these adults turning on the light bulbs, seeing that they had the ability to engage in academic work because they had already been successful in the job world. However, they'd chosen, for a number of life reasons to go back to school. They were very hesitant because they'd been out for ten, fifteen years. Their feelings about themselves were uncertain. Seeing them get excited, become confident, and decide to pursue more education, encouraged me to work even harder.

I'm now in a classroom situation where the average student is 18.3 years old. That's different from my community college mix where the average student age was thirty and had lots of experience. Now I'm dealing with students who don't have the life experiences but do have this unquenched optimism and wonderment about the world. So you change life experience for life expectation, and I enjoy that.

✑ Sonia Buckner

Sonia is thirty-seven years old and recently graduated from Alverno College.

I've always had trouble with just basic English and math. School was just difficult for me to take tests. I was always nervous when I was a kid, and I took that all the way up to my adulthood. Test taking was probably where I got all the sweaty palms and couldn't focus on things. In college life . . . I realized why I was having such a difficulty. I developed a learning disability and didn't know I had it. For all this time, for all these years, I had no way of understanding that because learning disabilities didn't come into play in my age group. It didn't come out until probably the later part of my years in college.

There are two teachers from my precollege days that I remember. There's a Mrs. Anderson and a person named Mr. Jackson. In high school I became pregnant. I was a teenage parent, and I went to a school that focused in on ladies who planned to still continue their high school education. These two teachers in particular they stand out with me because they pretty much were keeping me on focus in class. It was more of an individual basis the way they were teaching me. They took a lot more time, helped me to focus on my assignment and even looked beyond high school. They helped me look into the future ahead. They were more of a parent to me, telling me what to do and how to focus on the homework assignment. My principal found out I was pregnant and he called me at home one time. I remember this; he told me that he expected me not to be dropping out of school and to go ahead and continue on with my education. So he took the initiative on his half to call me; that stood out with me. To take the initiative was telling people that you're not just a number.

In college at first I was really embarrassed about receiving academic support because I didn't understand it. And it was kind of like a shame that I had some type of disability or anything like that or that I needed any special time outside with a tutor. Somehow they helped me to suppress that feeling about being embarrassed and stuff. They made me, not made me, but helped me to realize that it was so helpful for me and that I shouldn't be embarrassed. They helped me understand that everybody learns in a different way and many people need additional help. That made me start feeling comfortable and once I started getting comfortable with that, I was able to take assignments in class and focus more and complete my studies successfully.

❧ Jeanne L. Higbee

Jeanne is a professor and the faculty chair at the General College of the University of Minnesota. She has written a great deal and is considered a national leader in conducting and advocating for research in the field of developmental education.

At the University of Georgia, I had a student early on in my years there who had come from south Georgia as a football player. He already had a child, was maybe twenty-one when he started college and was just an incredible young man. He got to know my entire family. My parents got invested in seeing him do his thing too. It took him five years to graduate. His best buddy went on to play for the National Football League (NFL) and had a very, very successful career with the New York Giants for a long time and was very visible. And this guy was not physically large enough despite his skill to get a career in the NFL, so he went home because his mom needed him and taught in the high school from which he had graduated. He described that high school to me; I think this was part of what was so meaningful because this was in 1985 or 1986 and schools were supposed to be desegregated. Well, they had just gerrymandered the lines between the county school district and city school district so that the schools were still very much segregated. He came in just very weak, especially in things like math and writing. But he went on to become a teacher and then a police officer in Dallas.

The other student who had a huge impact on me was a student I met in the same time frame who had a learning disability and was brilliant. But this was back in the days when you had to fail a foreign language before they would consider exempting you from it. It was just so obvious that his learning disability was incredibly severe and yet he was so smart. He called me once from the Atlanta bus depot because he had read the schedule wrong, and his aunt and uncle had dropped him off at the bus depot in the evening when the bus wasn't due to leave until the morning. So it was 8:00 at night, and he was stuck in this not so great part of Atlanta and just didn't know what to do. I had taken my Dimetapp already and was ready to put my kids to bed, so my husband, who had no idea what this guy looked like, drove the 90 miles each way to the Atlanta bus depot to pick him up so he wouldn't have to stay there overnight. He got back to Athens and could not tell my husband how to get to his house. They had to go to the university and then try to figure out from there how to get this guy home. He ultimately did not graduate from the University of Georgia because he flunked too many courses like foreign language, but he did graduate from another school in the system. His first job out of college was as an advocate within the district attorney's office.

This idea that because somebody can't communicate in certain ways, or has organizational deficits, makes them somehow unworthy of a college education when this was a guy that in most class discussions could contribute things that were just on a different plane in terms of critical thinking skills than other students in the class. Brilliant, brilliant guy. Now he owns his own business.

◄? Calvin Mackie

Calvin is an associate professor of mechanical engineering at Tulane University. He was awarded the Distinguished Alumnus Award from the National Association for Developmental Education in 2004.

My initial memory of school is, it goes way back to prekindergarten when I participated in a program something like HeadStart, but I believe it was called HomeStart. A teacher used to come to my house once a week to work with me. I'll never forget, you know, cutting triangles and circles and learning all the different things that I eventually figured I would need in kindergarten. Then I jump from this HomeStart program to 3rd grade when I had a teacher that pushed me and helped me accomplish a lot of things that I didn't even know were within me.

That teacher realized that I had an aptitude for mathematics, and she actually worked with me separate from the rest of the class and pushed me ahead of the class. Because I was becoming bored with what the mathematics class was doing and at the pace the class was moving. And she really pushed me forward. Once I got to 4th grade, the teacher in 4th grade picked up where the teacher in the 3rd grade left off. By the time I got out of 4th grade, I was doing math at the 6th-grade level because of that teacher.

But once I got to the 5th grade, this was one of the worst experiences. This teacher didn't take any special interest in me as an individual and tried to make me fit the group. And by the time I got back into the 6th grade, my mathematical level was probably back, you know, with the group. And thank goodness, the teacher that I had in the 4th grade was also my 6th grade teacher. She picked up again and began to push me and by the time I got out of 6th grade, I was doing 8th-grade mathematics.

Another thing about my teacher in the 6th grade; my parents were pretty much not formally educated. My mother had a high school diploma, and my father dropped out of school in 8th grade. So when I got ready to go to junior high school, I wanted to go to junior high school where all my brothers and sisters and cousins had gone. And this teacher called my mother and said, "No, we don't think he should go to this junior high; we think he should go to this junior high because it is a better school even though he will have to catch two buses." My mother believed that teacher, and I went to that school. And there was another teacher there who really took an interest in me and followed me for three years. And then they sent me to a high school where another teacher took an interest and followed me all the way through to college. At every point, except the 5th grade, there was someone to say, "Hey. This is what you need to be doing."

As a student, as a young kid, I fought it the whole way. I didn't want to be ahead of the class. I didn't want to go to the junior high school where other students were not going. I wanted to go to the neighborhood school. Once I got into college, I realized that these people had pretty much played an instrumental role in getting me where I was. And, if they had not been there, I don't know where I would have ended up.

I guess there's an experience and pretty much a person that influenced my attitude toward school. The person is my father, and the experience is the fact that my father was uneducated and worked every day from sunup to sundown as a roofer. Even though he was very successful as a roofer, it was very, very difficult work. And, as a young kid, he would take me on the roof with him, and as I grew older I would have to do more of the difficult work as a roofer. He would always say, "You don't have to choose this. This wasn't a choice for me. This is what, this is the only thing I can do, but if you go to school, you can do more than this." And that hot sun and high humidity motivated me to do well in school.

That was one factor. Another factor was my teachers who told me, they made me believe that college was the natural extension for what I was doing in high school. It was never an instance where I had the opportunity to consider that I was not going to college. From the time I got to high school, my teachers were asking, "Where are you going to college? You need to go to college." So, for me, I just figured that's what I was supposed to do.

My first college was Morehouse in Atlanta, Georgia. The funny thing about college is that once I got to college, I would describe myself as very determined. And I was determined because they put me, I was placed into remedial reading because they said I wasn't reading at the level where I was supposed to be reading. And reading had always been a challenge for me because I came up in a house with no books. So, once I got to college, people used to make fun of, you know, the guys from Louisiana because of the way we spoke; the way we read and the tests. Our SAT scores were low, so they put us in remedial reading. So I just took that as a personal affront. It was a personal challenge to do well for me. I was just determined to do well and finish college. I didn't take it personally when I was told I needed to take the course. I took it personally the way people responded to the fact that I had to take the course. When they told me I had to take the course, it was almost with a relief because I knew that my reading ability wasn't the best it could be. Especially when I got to Morehouse and saw the way these guys were speaking and reading and just handling themselves with the King's English.

In college I had a teacher, and the great thing about this teacher was that he was always challenging me. He always called me, as a sophomore, "Doctor." And you know, people talk about speaking into an existence, and he always called me "Doctor" in class. You know, he pushed me and he pushed me, and he said, "We expect you to go for your highest degree." I had never even heard of a PhD when I entered college. I didn't even know what the requirements were or what you had to do. This instructor was Dr. Gordon, and he was the chair of the Math Department.

Another professor I had was Dean Blocker, and from the day I stepped on the campus at Morehouse College, he was just like a staunch supporter and mentor. And when he tested me and my reading score came back really bad, Morehouse was pretty much sure they were not going to accept me. He went to the admissions' office and fought for me and told them, "Just give this kid a chance." He was the first person who said, "You can do this." Because Morehouse is a special case; it is an all-Black, male private school. So you know it was somewhat intimidating. A lot of guys who were there came from an environment that I'd never even been in before; they came out of homes I'd never been in before. And Blocker was the one who always told me, "You know, we're teaching you and training you to speak before corporate leaders and kings and queens."

He got to know me through a summer program, a science program, and I attended that program the summer after my senior year in high school. It had about sixty young men. And that's when it was a very intimate environment, and that's where everybody used to joke and clown. He used to talk to all of us. He used to go around and ask the teachers about different students and how they were doing. You know, "What do you see in this student or that student?" And somehow, we just connected. And he saw my determination, and he just said, "Hey. I'm here for you." My goal in life is to be him.

College was personal for me. It was very personal because of these individuals who took an interest in me and never allowed me to put doubt in my mind. When I failed, they told me it was not, that it was not me. They didn't let me stand for that. So, college for me was very personal, and it met all my challenges and it challenged me; it stretched me.

◄ʔ Robin Remich

Robin has her master's degree in developmental studies and has worked in education for over twenty years. She is the manager of the Learning Center at Oakton Community College, Skokie campus.

There are a lot of reasons that cause students to drop out of school. Finances are a big one, I think, also time management. Not understanding what it takes to do well in their classes leads to dropout rates and some of the students find they either don't have the time for it or they don't make the time. Whether they are truly motivated to be there or are there for somebody else is important; for the younger students if they are there for their parents, that makes a difference to their level of motivation. If they are there for other reasons, if they are not ready to do it, then they can fizzle out; too many students being pulled in a lot of directions. That's what I see all the time. They are working full time, taking care of elderly parents, taking care of cousins and sick people. It's just amazing to see the range of directions they are pulled. Trying to juggle all of that frequently leads them to drop out or stop out. Sometimes they don't make good choices in the beginning about course load and the number of courses they can handle. Sometimes they want to do too much and don't face the truth about their abilities and where they need to start. I've seen students who have started and left to work at McDonald's for a few years and then come back as totally different people (stop outs). You know, five years later and now they want to be here; they have figured it out. When they really want to be here, they can do whatever it takes to get it done.

If you're not impacted by students in this field, then you shouldn't be in it. And you constantly learn from your students. There is one student who I met when I was a graduate student, and we still have a relationship. This is a ten-year relationship, actually. She was my age, but her life was so different from mine. When we connected, as me being a tutor and her being a student, I just became fascinated by her pathway and my pathway. She was a single mom with a teenager. She had a low income, and she had come from a family with primarily a single parent. She had a learning disability and she was coming back to college for a bachelor's degree as a thirty-five-year-old single woman who rode her bike to school every day, even in the rain.

She had tremendous motivation and a curiosity that just kept her going. I just admire that she didn't allow her obstacles to get in the way, and she just kept plugging away. So we are still in contact and she now is taking classes at the community college because she wants to get a master's degree in social work and she has a few deficits to make up in the social sciences. So, she has returned and there she is. I am still helping her, and she's still plugging away. And now she's a grand-mother. Her daughter had a child in high school, and you just look at all of that; it's so different from my own background, but she's probably touched me the most and opened my mind to differences and potential. Every day, every week, there are students that we learn from. I think a lot of it just comes by taking the time for them and listening to where they are and accepting where they are and creating a safe environment for learning and an environment where they can take risks.

◄ Gary Saretsky

Gary is the founder and first president of the National Association for Developmental Education.

Teaching today is fraught with challenges that people never had before. Schools are under pressure to do a lot of different things. And resources for schools are tremendously distracted; I mean, if you have to spend money on metal detectors at school doors and guards instead of tutors and teaching aids and having my ideal environment where there is one teacher for every twelve students. But it's not a lost cause. If it were a lost cause, I wouldn't have been in it. No. It's not a lost cause. There are kids who are going to succeed in spite of the schools and those who will succeed because someone took an interest and took them by the hand and coached them and counseled them. Someone who taught them some skills to help them survive and to reinforce that we care about them, at every level.

◄ Karen Patty-Graham

Karen is the director of Instructional Services at Southern Illinois University. She has held many elected leadership positions in the field of developmental education at the national and state levels.

I was the firstborn among many grandchildren, so I got lots of attention. People read me books; I enjoyed looking at books. I was the apple of everyone's eye, so I had lots of opportunities to learn things and go places and see things. I learned to love books and puzzles and problem solving. I idealized my 1st-grade teacher. I didn't go to kindergarten, so my first experience in school was my 1st-grade teacher. I idolized her and I wanted to grow up and be just like her, so my goal, career-wise, was always to be a teacher, just like Mrs. Lykke.

I was one of those kids who learned to read using Dick, Jane, and Sally. I remember sitting in small groups, and I remember liking it when I could sit next to the teacher. I remember the pride with which she sort of expressed how she thought of us as students and as children. I remember the pat on the head when you did a good job with reading; I think she was a real gentle person, a really kind person. I don't recall ever the experiences of her reprimanding anybody. I just remember sort of the glowing aura of her being a nice person and of wanting to please her and being recognized when I did please her.

That early experience has informed my career as I try to find the positives in students and employees. I try to think about their sensitivity to the situation. I try not to offend or to reprimand without coaching. I try to find the plusses in what students are doing, but still find ways to bring them along.

In my working with university students, there have been a couple of folks who had very rough backgrounds. A young man who had been in and out of jail and was trying to come to school to make something of himself; he had a really jaded perspective of what education was all about. And it was a challenge for me, but it was also an opportunity for me to try to help him develop some of those attitudes toward reading that would open doors for him. He hadn't ever read anything before other than things he had to read. He had barely picked up a newspaper. I made sure that he acquired the skills to read, and then I talked to him about some of the things you could learn from newspapers, magazines, and books. I put some of these materials into his hands, and it really stirred his curiosity; that was very rewarding and fulfilling for me, but I think it was even more so for him. He did go on and finish his college degree. I've lost track of him over the last few years, but I know that he was gainfully employed following his degree.

I feel very satisfied when students sort of light up when they realize that we've been talking about words that they now recognize in *TV*

Guide or newspapers. That tells me that they have been thinking about the vocabulary we've talked about, and they have been picking up something to read. They suddenly become aware that there are words there and ideas there that they hadn't thought about and they've been in front of them all the time, and suddenly they can do something with them. That's very rewarding and exciting.

◄ε Tiana Ellis

Tiana Ellis, a former developmental student at Olive Harvey City College of Chicago, has completed a law degree and has recently passed the Illinois State Bar Exam.

My kindergarten teacher influenced me the most. She is partly responsible for my being the person I am today. She told me at the early age of five that I had dedication, and that's what it takes to be successful in life. She was very nurturing and motivating. She got me prepared for elementary school, and I was accepted into a gifted school after leaving her class. I can really attest to everything I learned, I learned in kindergarten. Teachers should be engaged and motivated to learn. Teachers should make themselves available outside of class time. Students should feel from teachers that they are interested in their learning, not that this is just a job for them.

◄ε Tamu Wright

Tamu Wright, age thirty-three, is a former developmental student and is currently taking courses at Olive Harvey City College of Chicago, in addition to raising her family. She works as a teacher assistant at Dunne Academy, and plans to continue her higher education.

In elementary school, I could not stand any of my teachers. I thought they were all mean. I had such a bad attitude toward my teachers; I did little to no work, so I had to repeat the 6th grade twice. It wasn't until I went to high school and developed a good rapport with a teacher by the name of Mrs. Bettye Richardson who was caring and very encouraging to me. She also gave me self-confidence.

As a student at a community college, I am more focused now that I am older and realize that school is a serious matter. I am dedicated to my courses and so excited about learning. My best college experience is realizing that I can be successful. My advice to college teachers would be to not give up on students who are underprepared. Try to work with them as much as possible. Get to know your students by name; this means a lot to be called by name by your college teacher.

My mother also influenced my attitude toward school. I had perfect attendance throughout elementary and high school. I had to be deathly ill to stay home from school. School is a top priority with my mother. She stressed there is nothing you can do that is worth anything without an education. She strongly encouraged me to do my best.

Susan Clarke-Thayer

Susan was the director of the Learning Center at Suffolk University in Boston for many years. She is currently the associate dean of the College of Arts and Sciences. Susan was the primary advocate for and the editor of the NADE Self-Evaluation Guides *published in 1995 and now considered a standard resource in the field.*

Back in those early years, I had not only the high-risk students as a reading specialist, but I was also training tutors. I viewed what we were doing in the learning center as the tutors' first professional experience. So there was a lot of training for them, not only in tutoring but in adult learning theory and those kinds of things but also in what it is to achieve and what it is to have goals and dreams. Anyway, I had some wonderful experiences with those students who came to me as freshmen and left to graduate. Their journey was so outstanding to watch, let alone the journey of the high-risk students. I think these students, the tutors, got to me more because I didn't expect it. I expected to make a difference in the lives of the students who came in for help, but I didn't expect the difference it made to really good students.

Since then, the person who runs the learning center for me now, who reports to me, is one of those students who came back. And my director of advising is another one who came back as an adult and is also working for me. You know, I have seen them grow into adults and succeed. I've had the joy of watching it; they have made a significant impact on me.

❧ Martha Maxwell

Martha is truly a pioneer in the field of student support. She received her BA in 1946 and her PhD in 1960, and has mentored thousands of professionals. She has authored multiple books and articles that are considered to be classics in the field.

There are seven persons named Martha Maxwell: counselor, teacher, academic advisor, reading and learning disabilities specialist, researcher, administrator, and perennial student. I think there are a few other roles. Cheerleader ought to be included. I would say that perennial student and cheerleader are the most apt descriptions. We are dealing with students who come from backgrounds where success has not been part of their repertoire. They have not been encouraged; in fact, many of them have been discouraged in academia. So they feel they can't do it. Once you get them working, then I think you have to be a cheerleader and help them along that way.

I worked very hard in school. I did well in elementary and high school. When I got to college, I began by majoring in music and then I shifted to English and then to half a dozen fields and finally majored in psychology. I left school for a couple of years and came back and graduated with a split major in economics and psychology.

I remember not knowing what I wanted to do in college, so when I was a senior we had a unit in career planning. One of the things we read about was the role of the vocational counselor. I said, "Gee, that sounds like a great job. I don't know what I want to be. Maybe if I were a vocational counselor, I'd learn about a lot of fields and be able to make up my mind." Lo and behold, I did eventually become a vocational counselor, but that is just the way things fell.

When I had been a freshman, I had gone into vocational counseling myself. I only saw one person; he tested me and said, "You are an overachiever." In those days, they worried about a lot of things we don't worry about today. That kind of hurt. What he meant was that I was working harder than I should, and I was getting higher grades than I was capable of. I don't think people worry about that today, but in those days I felt sort of taken aback about it. For the next eight years, I refused to take any of the standardized tests. But I also took an interest test from him, and he said, "Your interests look like you should go into college teaching." So here is an overachiever going into college teaching.

My first job, which was at American University, was at a counseling center. I was trying to be a counselor but had worked at the University of Maryland's counseling center and in that period, it was right after the war, most of the people we worked with were returning GIs going back to college. Many of them, if not most of them, needed help in reading and study skills and how to study; I had some experience with them, so when I got to my first job, they said, "Oh by the way, Martha, we want you to teach a reading course." I thought, well I'm not about to say no because it was a job that paid $3000 a year for twelve months, and I needed it. So I ended up teaching a reading course which was an adult reading course in how to read faster . . . I guess I got interested in how students learn because of the jobs I was thrust into; those were the jobs one got placed in those days. Both in American University and later on when I went back to Maryland, I worked in their developmental education program teaching classes. That got me more interested in problems that students who have difficulties bring to college.

I helped GIs improve their reading. The director of the counseling center who was my mentor and had been teaching that class said, "Don't worry, Martha." And he handed me some three-by-five slips of paper where he had notes and he said, "Just take these. You can teach the course on that." I don't remember the text I used. There were some texts then, and they weren't quite appropriate for my class that ranged from a navy captain down to two Black students from the deep South who had not finished high school.

I went to Berkeley as a visiting associate professor from Maryland. There was a group of students at Berkeley, but I have met them at other places as well, and these were learning disabled students who were there as juniors and seniors. What was fascinating about them was how they managed to find interesting ways to compensate for their disability. Some of them would get the books at the beginning of the summer and read them before fall. Some of them would spend 20 hours on an assignment; some would totally avoid writing anything. One guy very ingeniously would scotch tape and paste his essays together, and he got caught because he was a graduate student in social work, and you had to write up your cases; you really couldn't tape them together.

And another one was a forestry major, very bright kid, and he just had a terrible time with reading and spelling. But he hired the secretary in the forestry department to type his papers. The forestry faculty had a lot of poor spellers, so she did well. This kid had very good ideas. One of his ideas was on reforestation in Africa. The professor took it, and actually did it. These students were not dumb at all, but they had difficulty expressing what they knew and could do in written words, papers. I have always had an admiration for learning disabled students because they work so much harder than anybody else.

CONCLUSION

The stories in this chapter demonstrate clearly, from multiple perspectives, the power of belief in students. Students and professionals alike recount the significance of individuals who believed in them enough to inspire them to achieve. Sometimes this belief is demonstrated through tough love and increased academic challenge inside the classroom. At other times it comes out through time spent with a student outside of class to simply listen to their dreams or help them practice their English skills or identify resources that will allow them to complete their education.

This concept of believing in students and their ability to achieve is not always readily accepted by students. Many of them, unfortunately, have more experience in a system that has failed them and has not demonstrated a belief in their abilities. By the time they come through the doors of higher education, they have expectations of failure and low self-concepts. Those educators who do make a difference in their lives purposefully create climates where students can feel safe, safe to take the risks that are necessary to lead eventually to achievement. Though there may be bumps along the way, they begin to trust that there is someone who cares for them and will support them for the long haul because they truly believe in them. This seems to be happening at a micro level, through individual educators, rather than at the more systemic level of formal education.

The stories in this chapter help to lay the foundation for chapter 3. In that chapter we move from the basic belief in students to ensuring that access is meaningful and does not simply result in a revolving door that reinforces students' often-preconceived notions of failure.

Chapter 3

Access: The Myth and Reality of the Revolving Door ❧

Just the opportunity to connect with somebody and figure out what education meant to them, I saw it could give them access and freedom that they never had before. Being able to *release the promise they have* is really pretty incredible. I think we do that most every day in this field. (Nancy Bornstein)

INTRODUCTION

This chapter addresses the myths and realities of access and the revolving door through the crucial question: "How do we ensure meaningful access?" The issue of access, while adhering to standards, is an ongoing debate between educators, administrators, and policy makers. We will see that early efforts to foster access for the underprepared resulted in a revolving-door syndrome. Students were admitted, but not supported; they foundered, gave up, and dropped out.

Sharon Silverman shares the consequences of the revolving door and its impact on the institution and society, both financial and societal. She describes developments, which supported the underprepared at her former institution. Robert McCabe stresses institutional responsibilities toward its citizenry, rapidly changing the competencies necessary to ensure success in the workplace.

Jeanne Higbee and David Taylor discuss the reactions of provisionally-admitted students to the General College's efforts to assist them and how the General College has been forced to limit the number of high-risk students that they admit, resulting in increased flexibility in the delivery of support. Martha Maxwell adds the idea of providing "rigorous courses that train them to think and reason," while Pat Cross sees a trend where community colleges will serve as "the open door to everyone." Gary Saretsky provides his perspective regarding institutional responsibilities for retention and how, initially, and to some extent even today, high schools are blamed for inadequately preparing students for college work. Many of our interviewees discuss the need for changes in how society views academic support in general, and how these changes will continue to impact access and retention.

We follow these stories by looking at the history of the revolving door, the institutional policy relating to the underprepared and provisionally admitted, and then conclude with several ways in which developmental education is defined and has evolved over the years, along with the population wishing to attend.

THE STORIES BEGIN

(We have kept the interview portions of the book informal, and, for the most part, have not adjusted the words to follow formal grammatical structure. Also in the interest of preserving a representative historical record, we have not altered either the language or contents of the stories to reflect our own views.)

◀ℓ *Sharon Silverman*

> *Sharon Silverman is the former director of the Learning Assistance Center at Loyola University in Chicago and a 1999 Fulbright Scholar. She has co-authored two books,* Learning and Development *and* Learning Assistance and Developmental Education.

You'd like to think that the revolving-door phenomenon is a problem because it negatively affects people's lives, which it does, but the reality of higher education is that, more so than affecting people's lives, it affects the bottom line economically for those institutions facing the revolving-door problem. Obviously both situations exist, but I think the emphasis on retention is as much economic as anything else. Institutions can't exist with the revolving door. Aside from individual disappointments, struggles, and frustrations, society has been greatly affected by the revolving door because we have people going after goals that they don't achieve, and then falling short.

The Bridge Program was our access program at Loyola. We had an advisory board of faculty members who also taught in the program, so that's how we addressed it: as a collaborative team of support staff providers and faculty members working together. Ultimately the faculty who taught in our program were not developmental education faculty; they were faculty from other departments and they'd each individually, and then as a team, decide what standards they were going to use for the grades. The faculty pretty much had autonomy in terms of deciding how they would do that. They prided themselves on not being loose with their standards, and then they were repeatedly amazed at the students' outcomes. So it wasn't a big issue because they had to remember that our developmental students at Loyola came from the top of their high school classes, that their schools were in low performing areas so they have all of these abilities and behaviors. When they were in situations where the bar was raised, they got themselves to meet the bar. So you know, in some ways, they were very different than the developmental students in some settings because of the selection process.

The misconception is that they're never going to make it. It's a waste of time. It's a lot of money and energy spent on a population of students who'd be better off in vocational training.

I would hope that monetary support for developmental students will grow. There's not an institution in the United States that doesn't have something in place to address developmental programs and academic support. During the 1970s and 1980s, funding was a priority for developmental programs, and now professional associations have raised the standard for the profession. If we want to ensure access and success, we must provide the finances for students in need. We will pay for this in the long run with underemployed or if we don't support educational opportunity when it is needed.

✍ Hunter R. Boylan

Hunter is the director of the National Center for Developmental Education at Appalachian State University. He has been the lead researcher in nationally recognized studies related to best practice for underprepared students. His latest book is What Works: Research-Based Best Practices in Developmental Education.

Pat Cross coined the term, "revolving door." At least, she wrote about it in *Beyond the Open Door.* I think that was one of the most marvelous things that she ever did, talked about the "door" becoming the "revolving door." Once you put a name on it, it embarrasses people. Of course, university administrators don't like to be embarrassed. I was a university administrator back when they tried to keep this stuff in the closet. Under an open admissions policy, we're simply recycling people. They got even more embarrassed when the press and their legislators and the literature of higher education began pointing it out.

Many university administrators thought, "Well, fine. That's what we're here for, to weed people out. Keep all the best and the brightest maintaining the sanctified status of being a degree holder from our illustrious institution." I think in the community colleges it had a much different effect. There are a lot of people who believed they really were supposed to cater to the needs of the community for an educated citizenry, both the advantaged and disadvantaged people of their communities.

The self-concept in the community colleges is often, "These are last-chance institutions. This is where you go, and we have to take you in." I can't prove this; it's an opinion rather than fact. The stark contrast of what the community college stands for and what the "revolving door" stood for really made a difference on the way people perceived the institution, thought about it, and acted. That's why I think Pat Cross's work is so important; it put a name on something, and not a very nice name. It described the phenomenon that a good portion of our higher education system had to respond to. It's too inconsistent with the community college philosophy not to.

◄? K. Patricia Cross

Pat Cross is professor emerita of higher education at the University of California, Berkeley. She has authored ten books and over two hundred articles and has lectured on American higher education in the United States and Europe. She is currently a trustee of the Carnegie Foundation for the Advancement of Teaching and the Berkeley Public Library.

I'm not absolutely sure that the phrase "revolving door" originated with me. I talked primarily about the "open door" in the 1970s when community colleges were being established at the rate of one a week. The implication of *Beyond the Open Door* is that there had to be more to education than access. I wasn't as much focusing on people going in and out as I was trying to get people to focus on the progress we were making in *educating* students. I felt we needed to pay attention to what that access to higher education accomplished. How good was the education? What were the learning experiences? So, I don't know that I would take credit for the promotion of the term or concept of the revolving door. I don't know whether it's in my writing or not, but in any case, I think what I wanted to get at was: What happens after you pass the access barrier?

Access is certainly important; I thought it was important thirty years ago, and I still think it's critically important. I think it is not *all* that is important. What I am afraid of is that researchers are studying questions of policy, that is, they are trying to tell legislators what they ought to do about making access available to people, and certainly that is the first step. But, I think that we ought to be going beyond that to asking, "OK, once they get access, what are we doing in terms of learning?" And that's the next step I've always been interested in. I think we ought to be thinking about all those people who are gaining access now, and what we are doing for them in terms of learning.

I guess the most common misperception probably is that quality and access are incompatible with goals for excellence and education. People used to think that "open admission colleges" could never be as "good" as research universities.

I think that we have made significant progress as more people get some personal experience with community colleges. We know that many people who have not previously done very well in school are capable of doing extremely well. There is also a growing perception that the narrow range of academic talents is not all we need in an open society. We need people, for instance, who are very sensitive and work well with other people. We need people-oriented skills; we have not even approached that in higher education, yet more people lose their jobs because they can't get along with people than because they can't do the technical work of their job.

◄ζ Martha Maxwell

Martha is truly a pioneer in the field of student support. She received her BA in 1946 and her PhD in 1960 from the University of Maryland and has mentored thousands of professionals. She has authored multiple books and articles that are considered to be classics in the field.

Berkeley didn't really have a "revolving door," but it took a lot of students who were not qualified and they didn't last too long. So there was a question of retention. Actually, they gave them more services in the 1970s. It was clear that Berkeley was doing a better job than many state universities in terms of training and graduating minorities. It put a lot of effort into it and did what it could to help the students.

Berkeley had a strong learning center; they had a well-coordinated program that involved everything from placement to financial aid. They nurtured the students when they got admitted; it was a question of identifying them early. In the 1960s, they would just bring them in. The student would get a letter saying, "You are a special admit," which didn't mean anything to the student. Then another letter said "Come on in and see somebody," which they would not do. But when they began to organize this effort and get the students in who needed help, it was much more effective. I still believe that if you tell students they need help, or if you think they know they need help, they will volunteer; that is not the way it works. Most likely, they will run to the other end of campus before they will seek help.

A lot of southern states, particularly, mandated testing and remedial courses. But there are always problems with a mandated program that involves forcing students into a program. There is really no one way, one best way, to deal with underprepared students. From a faculty point of view, if you can assign them to a course and get them out of your office, you are fine. That is cheap and quick. I personally feel it would be better if we took a stand on underprepared students now that we are getting down to the bottom and say, "look, if you are going to college, take college prep." For many of our students, in particular the third that are required to take our courses, have not had the regular college prep program. I don't think you can do that in one semester or with a course or two. They need the rigorous courses that train them to think and reason. We are kidding ourselves if we think we can help them quickly get up to par when they haven't had three or four years of this back when they could learn it more readily. Besides, you have the attitudinal problems when they are in college and have gotten by without having had these courses.

Today we are getting students in the bottom 20 percent coming to college, and a lot of students from ESL backgrounds where English is not spoken at home, refugees and that sort of thing; they need developmental education.

It is almost as if there is a great wall between high school and college people. The college people don't go down and talk to the high school folks unless they happen to get a grant or have a special program that lasts six months; they never endure. There is a bar in terms of high school people chatting with college instructors to really explore these ideas, getting them out on the table, and talking about what you do about it. There are places where learning specialists at the college level go down to high schools and work with the students and get them ready. That's the kind of preparation we should have more of, but it is not on most people's list of tasks to do this week.

I think it is inevitable [relegating developmental education to two-year colleges] as we get more students in college, because with very few exceptions, four-year college budgets are not growing. They have increased every year since World War II. The public is saying, "No more." They are willing to increase budgets for two-year colleges. That sort of puts the four-year college in a position where they have to be more selective about students; they can't take everybody. And I think that will exacerbate the problem of underprepared students going to a four-year college and will help them to begin to shift more to two-year schools. I think it will hit the two-year schools too; they will probably become more selective.

I would like to see prep schools develop so that can get students back on track. Somebody has to say sooner or later to high schools, "Look, you have got to do a better job because these students, whether you like it or not, are going to go to college." In other countries where they have greater problems with articulation, they do have opportunities for adults, for students who haven't mastered their high school courses, to go back for a college prep year. We do it for the service personnel, and those have been successful programs. It seems to me that it makes more sense than taking a reading course if you are weak in reading, or a reading and a math course because you need to have some content to broaden your background; it could be incorporated in the high school level.

Back in the old days, in the 1930s when I went to high school, there were students who wanted to go to college and really couldn't quite make it. So they stayed on in high school and took a post-graduate year, which was the same thing. I remember that they did well when they got to college, but they needed that extra year. We just have a feeling that if you are an adult you ought to go to college; you ought not to stay in high school. And that is sort of a belief that isn't really necessarily true. And in the old days, too, a lot of colleges had high schools attached to them where they trained teachers and prepared students; we have let go of that kind of training.

◄ℓ Gary Saretsky

Gary is the founder and first president of the National Association for Developmental Education.

We touched the nontraditional student who now is the typical student: Students going on to college were underprepared. They couldn't pass; they had insufficient skills. They didn't have the reading skills to succeed. A majority of these kids graduated from high school, and when you consider one-third of the kids who went into high school didn't graduate from high school, the population was pretty representative.

My doctorate was in instructional design and development, so I knew the things that should happen for people to learn and about learning. And you knew that wasn't happening in higher education. That was a secondary agenda. No one ever got a promotion, I shouldn't say no one, but rarely in the university setting did people get promotions for winning "teacher of the year" award. They got promoted because of publications and grants. Maybe in the community colleges teaching was a prime mission. But it wasn't in higher education, or at the doctoral levels, or in most four-year institutions. Teaching wasn't necessarily the prime focus of many schools.

So, you had a whole group of people who came in, and it used to be that the freshman year was the sorting mechanism of separating the wheat from the chaff, those who could survive, and those who could not. It was never a place where, until the freshman year programs started, it was important to retain students.

But there were a few institutions, before there was a wave of financial constraint on many institutions, where their survival was based on enrollment and retaining students. Until that happened, they said the freshman year is basically where we flunk out a certain percentage of kids, and you grade on a curve. And those who make it, on their own, are going to come out on top and those at the bottom, tough luck. Then they started the freshman year experience that began to increase retention. After that, you had the federal programs. Then they had educational opportunities programs all designed to take nontraditional students and help them survive.

This was all happening in the 1970s, right when I was active in the field. The door was open and it was revolving. Students were going in and dropping right off. There was a big book on the revolving door, where people were going in and they were being tossed right out and wasting a year. And you ended up being crushed, your self-esteem crushed. The institution never assumed responsibility. They were always pointing the fingers at the high schools for not adequately preparing them. And, of course, the high schools turn around to the junior high schools and say you guys aren't doing the right job. And they in turn blame the elementary schools.

✊ Nancy Bornstein

Nancy is the director of the Learning Center at Alverno College, a liberal arts college for women nationally known for its innovative competency-based curriculum and system of assessment. She served as the president of the National College Learning Center Association and was co-editor of The Learning Assistance Review.

We purposely accept many students who will find college challenging. That's part of our mission. Students are required to take developmental courses if they don't meet specific assessment criteria. Sometimes students are upset or angry and say, I studied that in high school. I shouldn't have to do this. We teach our classes in a way that's really different from what they experienced in high school. They start to see what we're asking for. What we're working with them on is being able to perform at a level of reading, or writing, or quantitative work, which really *is* different from what they did before. They're not doing it over.

We have a system where students can take a leave, and the advising office formally keeps in touch with them when they take a leave. They have to formally declare that this is what they're doing; they can't just disappear. Some do, and if they disappear, then they have withdrawn and then can return. So, we try to set up a system where it's not hard to come back. They can return up to four semesters later without re-applying. It's called "student on leave."

A very large percentage of our students are first-generation college students, which means they're not coming out of backgrounds where people are familiar with college or what's behind some of the things you study, so I think they can have a lot of motivation and a lot of ability but it's not connected.

But, at times, what we're seeing is some of those students have more complex issues that affect them and thus affect them in the classroom and affect their learning. That's something we're struggling with.

Just the opportunity to connect with somebody and figure out what education meant to them, and how they really saw it could give them access and freedom that they never had before. I've always believed in that, but, that shifted my view of education and why I think working in this field is so critical. Being able to *release the promise they have* is really pretty incredible. I think we do that most every day in this field. I think a lot of teachers do that, but it's more of a struggle to do it here.

~ David V. Taylor

David is the former dean of the General College at the University of Minnesota. While there, he promoted new initiatives and helped to develop a nationally recognized research base for the College. David was active professionally in the community surrounding the University and has led several research projects investigating ways to support disadvantaged youth. He is currently the vice president of Academic Affairs at Morehouse University.

There is the notion that we at the University of Minnesota General College are the flagship, and because we are the flagship, and are known internationally for the research here, that we ought to be accepting only those undergraduates who hold exceptional promise. At the same time, we are a land grant institution, and our mission is to work with the use of the state funds in order to deliver a high-quality education to everyone.

That doesn't mean that only certain social and economic classes of people would apply. We have been adamant about having ordinary citizens, but it is students who may not meet the profile that we're after, still having the opportunity to access the university and to compete. So, it helps having that as our mission. Against all odds, there have been attempts to close the General College. We were looked upon, at one point, as being kind of the remains of a bygone era of liberality. We've maintained that we are, in fact, doing what the state would require us to do in achieving a level of access. (Note: In June 2005, the General College *was* eliminated as a separate unit of the University of Minnesota.)

Having said that, the compromise has been that we admit only 875 students a year, out of an incoming class of about 5,000. We will be forced to reduce that to about 10 percent of the incoming class in the next couple of years to placate those who are concerned that perhaps we are still admitting too many average students. And we have limited the number of high-risk students that we work with now. We still admit these students on an experimental basis. But reluctantly, we have come to realize that as our preparation standards advanced, we have to be a little bit more flexible in order to meet expectations. So, it's a dance that we do, a very sophisticated, ritualistic dance, but we've been able to do it and maintain access here.

✎ Robin Remich

Robin has her master's degree in developmental studies and has worked in education for over twenty years. She is the manager of the Learning Center at Oakton Community College, Skokie campus.

Tuition is going up. Financial aid is currently going down. You know, there are going to be supposedly more traditionally-aged students going to college, so that cohort is growing. And, it does bring with it the challenges of diversity, including a lot of language diversity; Hispanic students growing, students who in the past would have never considered higher education are going.

So, the challenge of how to deal with, or how to respond to those needs and where to respond to those needs, whether that's going to be all institutions or institutions like community colleges. Is that going to be the place where all developmental students are going to go?

I think each state is handling those issues differently at this point. We have also seen an increase, I think, from our personnel who deal with students with disabilities . . . of more psychiatric disabilities. And, there is the sense that with more medication and more services for that population at a younger age, and the awareness of Americans with Disabilities Act, and those students getting services in high school . . . they are demanding the same services from the postsecondary institutions. There's a challenge there: Are they truly learning disabled? Or are they developmentally disabled, where across the board they are low functioning? That is a population that, I think, it's hard to know how to serve, to determine where they need to go. Overall, I think that could be a national issue.

◄₹ Jane Neuburger

Jane is the director of the Learning Resource Center at Syracuse University. She currently chairs the National Certification Council for the National Association for Developmental Education.

I think we also have a responsibility to the institution of not passing students, or not promoting students who really are not going to make it in college. That very well may have been what happened to us in the 1970s. If, in the top level of developmental writing you are held to standards of how many people passed the course, then a lot of people are going to pass the course. On the other hand, if your assessment is based on how many people, of those who successfully complete, are going to successfully complete a college level writing course, then you have that dual role of maintaining standards while providing access.

That may not be more true for community colleges than elsewhere but, like it or not, it was very true at Cazenovia (small private college). If the students there needed to learn to write better or to read better, that's fine. But, if the reason for the uppermost developmental course is preparation for the next course, which I think is true, then those students who aren't ready, ought not to be passed along. They need to receive that message and that is a hard, hard line to hold.

I think that we have more support from our faculty colleagues than we might think when we present a role in those two ways. We are here to support the students and help them, but we are also here to help maintain institutional standards.

Some people need a little bump up; a little help. And for other people, the lightbulb comes on. Still other people just are really not going to make it. That doesn't mean, even if they fail the class, that they haven't learned something. We need to figure out how to measure that, particularly at the community college level. Have you increased your literacy? So, you are reading now. You came in reading at the 4th grade level, and now you are reading at the 8th grade level. That's great. Does that make you college ready? Well, I don't know. You can write a business memo, but you can't write an essay.

◄៩ Juele Blankenberg

Juele, now retired, was the manager of Tutoring Services at Oakton Community College in Illinois. She frequently taught graduate courses in the field of developmental studies.

Access (at Oakton Community College) doesn't seem to be a problem if you are talking about access to developmental education because we have that whole placement system in the works. You know community college persistence isn't as clean and tidy as perhaps a residential school might be because many will only come to school every fall or every spring, and they stop in and stop out. If you are looking at persistence as in, "are students registered every semester?" or something like that, it might be disappointing. But if you look at longitudinal studies and advancement of a particular student, you have a better picture of what persistence might be.

◄៩ Susan Clarke-Thayer

Susan was the director of the Learning Center and is currently the associate dean of the College of Arts and Sciences at Suffolk University in Boston. Susan was the primary advocate for and the editor of the NADE Self-Evaluation Guides published in 1995 and now considered a standard resource in the field.

If we're really committed to equality and affirmative action, civil rights and all of that, then, you have to do more than just integrate the schools. And, that's kind of what happened in the 1970s. You have to level the playing field, so that high-risk students have a way to overcome the disadvantages. I think that's where developmental education came in. It's just that when it first came in, nobody knew how to do it particularly. I mean, now we're so much clearer. And, of course our leaders in our field have been saying all the right things. Georgine Materniak (professional colleague of Clarke-Thayer) and I had reread Keimig, her vision for developmental education, holistic and that kind of thing. It was so right on target even way back then, but we weren't doing it. We had to come to the point to understand that we have the responsibility to get rid of the revolving door by providing the appropriate support, not crutches but support, so that students learn those skills and strategies and compensation techniques that can allow them to become independent, successful learners.

I think that politics are still evolving. Mandatory placement, we more or less have it, although if a student absolutely refuses, we don't dismiss them or anything. We make strong recommendations. You wait for the teachable moment because a lot of times in higher education, anything that has to do with assessment in any way is incredibly threatening and just negative. It's just not a popular notion. But, there are techniques, concepts for trying to get at it, which are supported by research, and you hear and how other institutions are using it.

We ran into a big problem with second language students; it was discovered that in our efforts to have access, admissions was admitting students who really couldn't read and write English very well. We didn't have anything in place to catch that and help them.

So, large numbers of these students were flunking out right and left. In other cases they had managed to get by if there was no in-class writing; it was becoming pervasive, and the whole thing blew up. That provided the groundwork for saying, "It would really help if we could test these students using placement tests. It would help us place them in the right services and the right English classes they would need."

Eventually the time became right. We tried to move the placement tests into a standard model where a team reviews the writing samples. It is not done in the English class; it is done in the summer during orientation so that the registrar places students into appropriate courses. Then we brought out the idea of doing math placement and got the math department involved, and now we have that as well.

Articulation agreements are becoming increasingly common. We do have the students take the placement exams though. We want everybody to take the placement exams. This helps the honor students as well, because then they can be placed into honors classes.

This particular school, Suffolk University, started out very much focused on access in a kind of unique way because it's not a community college; it's a four-year college. There are a couple of doctoral programs, and the place is growing considerably. But, its roots are ... in the original school back at the turn of the century, you know, 1906. It was a law school that was started in somebody's living room. Because in Boston, back then, only the Boston Brahmins could go to law school ... to Harvard and the schools around here. So, the Irish, the Italians, all the immigrants, were not accepted to those schools. This guy started a law school for people who couldn't go to the others because he felt that it was discrimination and that it was ridiculous. They should have an opportunity to be attorneys just like everyone else, so that's what the school is grounded in, that "access and opportunity" tradition.

On the other hand, the faculty really wants higher quality students, and the SAT scores have been going up. Now we're looking at access in a couple of different ways: one is diversity. It's ensuring people from all different backgrounds, cultures. We have a truly diverse population here since we've brought so much through internationalization. The other thing we have is a very strong conditional admissions program. It's been designed by our learning center. Students who are admitted through it, the faculty can't complain about, because the program is so good. Those students succeed and when they leave it, you can't tell the difference between students who have been in the program and those who have not. Whereas before, for years, we had a conditional admit program that had no conditions, this one does. So, we do offer access through that and also through our second language programs.

We have an ESL program where we have special admission that lets students come in and have their first year sheltered. That's also very well-rounded, very successful. We have an English Language Institute, but that's noncredit bearing. The ESL program is for credit, but it is possible for students to come here and take the English Level I prior to applying. Both of those programs are access programs. The learning center and the developmental programs take a holistic approach. Anybody from any kind of background or need finds a support service here using a holistic approach, as long as they get in, and it's not that hard to get in. But the thing is can they stay in?

⁂ Karen Patty-Graham

Karen is the director of Instructional Services at Southern Illinois University. She has held many elected leadership positions in the field of developmental education at the national and state levels.

Let me step back for a little bit . . . I did my higher education in the state of Illinois in 1965–1969. At that time, there was a plethora of students wanting to get into higher education, so at least my institution, Northern Illinois University, a state institution, could afford to be somewhat selective in who it took into the university. I think that moving into the 1970s, we didn't have quite that level of selectivity in higher education, as there were more opportunities for students to get into higher education with community colleges opening up, more opportunities for students in higher education, and certainly with the federal grants that students could have to get into education.

I think, in the 1970s, we were not set up to help those students who came into higher education who had not been afforded the opportunities before. Because in the 1960s, we didn't, as institutions, I think, put much emphasis on closing the gap for students who were new to education, so I think the revolving door existed to a great extent in the seventies, where students were being let in, brought in, encouraged, as there was more marketing to get that piece of that action for students.

As the numbers of high school students dropped, there was more competition, so four-year institutions were sort of forced into taking students they wouldn't have taken otherwise. But, there really wasn't the emphasis on what to do with them. I think some of the TRIO programs, the special services programs that came into being in the 1970s, started to point out that for some students we needed to close the gap. At Southern Illinois University (SIU), Edwardsville, we started out with the Experiment in Higher Education, that was what it was called, back in the mid-60s to early 1970s. And, it was only at our East St. Louis campus. East St. Louis was a heavily minority city, and so that's where the need was recognized first. We saw that maybe the education that the students brought to higher education was lacking, and so there was a need to fill in some of the blanks. That program was eventually brought to our main campus in the late 1970s.

When I started at SIU, Edwardsville, in 1976, I moved into our supplemental services program in, I guess it was 1980, and we were trying to do something about closing that "revolving door." As an institution, we sort of had an open admissions policy for every term except for fall term. Fall term—that was when we wanted to have the numbers that were high ACTs and all those sorts of things. But, we were pretty much an open door for the other terms. However, there was always that competition for students, and so you always let in a few more students than you would have otherwise, but we had a program in place to deal with those students. We have gotten wiser in higher education over the years, so that if you look at the research and the literature, you would see that about 80 percent of four-year institutions have developmental programs or some sort of developmental services for students.

In Illinois, we have the community college system, and we talk about eliminating developmental education from four-year institutions so that they aren't open-door institutions. Instead, we talk about sending those students to the community college, which then turns the community college into the revolving door. Now even some of the community colleges are saying: "We can't deal with the numbers of students who are coming in here, and we're going to have to look at whom we're going to admit and what the quality is of those students that we admit." So, I think in some ways, some of those doors are beginning to close as we reach the higher numbers of students who are graduating from high school. I guess we'll continue along that rate, until about 2008 is my understanding, and then the high school population will tend to decline. Then I think we'll be in a competitive mode.

I think that "revolving door" relates to the clientele that's out there, the numbers that are out there, the marketing that institutions look at to market who they are, and what they think they are, through their clientele. I think there's an economic issue related to that revolving door. And, it will continue to revolve in some institutions and for some students. But, I think that as long as there are programs to support students who attend the universities and colleges, we'll be doing something to try to close that revolving door.

◄₂ Dana Britt Lundell

Dana directs the Center for Research on Developmental Education and Urban Literacy (CRDEUL) at the General College of the University of Minnesota. She is the author of numerous articles and coedits the CRDEUL monograph series.

I understand the concept of "revolving door," but it's funny because I feel like I'm so new obviously, in my work in developmental education, although I've almost been at it ten years considering when I stepped into General College. The metaphor actually makes sense. It seems like we're letting people in but then not providing the support, so they go right back out, so persistence levels are low.

We just did a study with Hennepin County. Dean Taylor led part of a county-wide team that wanted to look at African American males between the ages of eighteen and twenty-four from Hennepin County and what happens to them in terms of going through the educational system. But, more broadly, they looked at all sorts of areas, economic and social. It was a real multilayered study. Our little piece of it just looked at General College data, University of Minnesota admissions data, and tried to identify what happens to students from this population that come into the college, and a lot of them come through General College.

There are very few African American males admitted to the University of Minnesota. It's so embarrassing; the statistics are terrible. The university needs to know about this. As we were starting to look at this, we began to talk about it. I know there have always been overt conversations at General College about what happens when our students transfer into programs and what is the follow-up; if they're getting a supportive learning environment here that says it's about multiculturalism. And they're getting a lot of that support here. Isn't there a responsibility in other parts of the university for the same exact issues we overtly take responsibility for? We keep asking, so, what happens? Do they drop out? What's happening when they go into the Institute of Technology? Yeah, they go into General College, but who's transferring? Who's graduating? As they begin to attack us, there are questions about that.

We want to turn the tables in saying, "Yes, we take some responsibility, and here's what we're doing," but this is about all that happens with all first-year students. What is the climate in various departments? I think the things that we talk about overtly in developmental education are issues for *all* programs. But, it's so hard to convince other departments of that. They think that old model is fine, and we just push them back out the revolving door. Who let *you* in? You know.

David V. Taylor

David is the former dean of the General College at the University of Minnesota. While there, he promoted new initiatives and helped to develop a nationally recognized research base for the College. David was active professionally in the community surrounding the university and has led several research projects investigating ways to support disadvantaged youth. He is currently the vice president of Academic Affairs at Morehouse University.

In the late 1960s, early 1970s, the government passed legislation designed to offer financial aid and make access to higher education more affordable. It was looked upon as a form of national defense: if we were going to prosper as a nation, if we knew higher education was the root by which we could develop a very literate and highly skilled workforce, then it was in the interest of the government to make that access possible.

A number of people were encouraged to go to school; institutions were encouraged to expand to receive these students, and the programs were being sponsored through the agency of the government. These were to help people acquire skills necessary to complete their educational training. The concern wasn't, in at least many institutions, so much who is graduating, but the monetary resources, the financial resources that these students brought. So, if at the finance level you could bring in a lot of students who could provide streams of revenue, there wasn't really a lot of thought given to retention.

That became a highly dubious proposition. We weren't really about student success, or providing access. So there was a notion of "revolving door:" "We'll give you an opportunity to show whether or not you are made of material that succeeds, and if you don't succeed, well it was a noble effort, on to the next body."

At the University of Minnesota we were kind of involved in that from a very altruistic kind of perspective. We had a series of programs designed to bring people of color, women, and people from poor socioeconomic backgrounds into the university. We had something called the HELP Program (Higher Education for Low-income People, initiated in 1967); and the Progress Education Program, PEP it's called, and that was for students of color, giving them support, and recruitment support to careers. That was designed to open the door for opportunities to low-income people of color, programs for people on public assistance. All of those things were done in an altruistic fashion, but the end result was a revolving door. The people did not get degrees; they were very disenchanted with higher education, and we were wasting both financial resources and human resources.

◄₹ Jane Neuburger

Jane is the director of the Learning Resource Center at Syracuse University. She currently chairs the National Certification Council for the National Association of Developmental Education.

In the early 1970s, I graduated from college. I was working in junior high and then in high school, and then I had children, so I wasn't in college in any way, shape, or form, in the 1970s. What I think, though, is that having heard so much about the "revolving door," and talking it over with colleagues, it had a negative impact on developmental education. Prior to that time, historically, there were tutors available. There were tutors available in Harvard. There were college preparatory courses. If you weren't quite ready to attend university, you could go to preparatory school.

I think there were a lot of tutoring models like that. I think the GI Bill and the guaranteed student loans opened the floodgates to having a lot of students at colleges and universities. Then, those colleges and universities needed to expand and realized that they had a whole huge array of preparation, both strengths and weaknesses, in their students. I really think that the GI Bill and the guaranteed student loans did that.

I don't know whether, in the 1970s, the revolving door was a backlash to "Hey, there're a lot of these students who shouldn't be here, but we need them here because now we created a huge number of community colleges and smaller colleges." But I think that we, developmental educators and the field itself, took a hit on that. I think we began to be seen as the barrier; if you are in developmental education, you really aren't supposed to be here anyway. So, part of your job is, "Don't let these people in. Put them in other classes, but let's not let them in *real* classes." I really don't know where that was coming from. My guess would be from inside the academy and outside; a little bit of both.

There's always a movement, there's always a tension, I think in any college or university, and the whole culture of higher education of maintaining the old ways, which would mean we would still be teaching Latin and Greek, and accommodating the new students.

I think it's appropriate for that struggle to happen in higher education, and at the university level because that's where it needs to be hashed out, so that we are sure that we do keep the best of the old and yet incorporate the new, as well. I think that is appropriate. I think developmental education, though, probably took a hit on that.

We work with *those* students. We hear, "*Those* students don't belong here, anyway." We "do the homework for them." We "write the papers for them." There's that side, the cry that we are helping *too much*. I think that that's a common misperception. I think equally as strong is the perception that we are not helping enough particularly in learning assistance and tutoring. As a tutor coordinator I used to hear both of those complaints. "Well, this person wrote a paper and worked with a tutor. How come this paper isn't better?" You should have seen it before! And also, "This person worked with a tutor, and this paper is much better than it ever was before, so the tutor must have written it." So, I think that those are two sides of the misperceptions of what we do. We do *too much*. We don't *do enough*.

Maybe we should substitute an elevator for the revolving-door metaphor. Some students should have a successful trip to the first floor, which might represent increased literacy skills; others might travel to the second floor and a 24-credit certificate. Others might head for the penthouse and a PhD.

❧ Gladys Shaw

Gladys is the retired program director for Student Support Services at the University of Texas at El Paso. She has been very involved at the national level in setting standards of practice for academic support services in colleges and universities.

Well, I think the "revolving door" was sort of based on that elitist perception that, "Ok, we'll give them a chance, but if they don't make it the first time, then out they go," kind of thing. When they did that here, they would only take provisional students one semester of the year. And, if they didn't make it, they were out. And, it was only, I think, when we got the antipoverty, and when we got the emphasis, and we got the funding. When the federal funds came down, then people began to pay more attention to it. And, I really and truly think that the revolving door was a big part of our whole retention program and why universities weren't graduating a high percentage of their students. Unless they were just . . . you know if they had those students, and they didn't keep them, then in comparison to the total students . . . it looked really bad.

Initially there weren't any support systems, so, it was just either, "You make it on your own or else you're outta here." Many of them were not even here. The college didn't have orientation and advising; at one point, we put in a plan for these kids. Nancy Wood was instrumental in that; she was in the Tutoring and Learning Center here at that time and had worked with us in the Upward Bound Program.

Having worked in the Upward Bound Program, we knew that these interventions worked. Upward Bound was very, very big on writing, reading, study skills, and math. Nancy Wood came to us and took over the tutoring center. She worked with somebody from the math department and somebody from the registrar's office, and we put in a program of orientation, advising, study skills; we had a tutoring program. But the first few semesters that it was in place they had phenomenal success in keeping these students, and they were keeping hardly any of them before. And, by keeping more of them, well, now they bemoan the fact that maybe only half of them persist, but when you compare that with nothing, that was pretty good.

If they came in under the START Program, or, at that time it was called the "Provisional Admission Program," they were required to take nine credits of study skills class. Eventually, students were required to come to orientation, and advising was required. Now, all the students, the General Studies' students that have declared a major, are required to do this. General Studies' students, I believe, are not required to do orientation. The provisional students are, but they have sold it so well that I think about 90 percent of the kids coming in do participate in orientation.

I think it should be required, and I think it should be more than a couple of days. As far as I'm concerned, the whole first semester could be considered an orientation. And, I think that's kind of what we've got here because they did away with our study skills class and replaced it with the university seminar. Study skills is supposed to be a part of that, and that's not working very well. But, they may change that. So, for my program . . . I'm still asking our students to go through our study skills class.

The university seminar class is an academic, theme-based, core requirement for all students now. A professor proposes an academic theme, and there are small classes; they have an instructor, and then they have a peer leader. It's a good model, but so many of the professors don't have a clue about study skills. Once they're teaching in that program "that taught study skills" for me, those kids get study skills. But, one of our best professors on campus said, "I don't know how to teach that," and, he's a novelist. He's a wonderful history professor. But, he just said, "I don't know how to do that."

So, they come into our program designed for first-generation, low-income students with academic needs. We still have two study skills classes: critical reading, and the other is study skills, and they are both noncredit. We always look at all students to see what they need, but most of them go through those two classes. We cluster those two classes with an academic course so that we're combining study skills and Supplemental Instruction (SI), so they get the feel of how to really deal with this information.

The student population here is primarily Hispanic. I don't have the latest numbers, but I know we're probably 70 percent to 80 percent Hispanic, maybe not quite that much. I think they're probably twenty-three, twenty-four years old. Most of them receive financial aid, and a lot of them work. I would say thirty percent to 50 percent of them work. It's hard to know from one semester to the next. We discourage students from working as much as we can because we want them to succeed here, but sometimes it just can't be helped; they have to work. Some of them come in as provisionally-admitted students. That may be changing because we have an initiative going on with the high school to prepare students for college, setting goals, determining what courses they need, and that kind of thing. So, that may change in time. It may get less, I hope.

We get quite a few students from the bilingual program. Some come over ready to handle English. But, you hardly hear English anymore outside of class because we're right here on the border. And, our president is very committed to serving the population that we have: the community.

◄¿ *Robert McCabe*

Bob is a senior fellow with the League for Innovation in the Community College and a former president of Miami-Dade Community College.

I have to go back to the 1960s, I think, to comment about the 1970s. I've been around since before dirt, so I've got all this background. In college, in the 1960s, we (and I participated) let people take anything they wanted. We were into, "You're all right; I'm all right. You do your thing." Everyone knows better what they can do than we do, don't put any hurdles in anyone's way. We had as clear a consensus in this country as I think we've ever had on the issue of trying to, in effect, remediate the conditions that minority people had growing up in this country, and trying to bring more equity. And in that condition we let people move through the system without very much guidance; you know, without the same expectations that we should have had. And if I could reset my head back to about 1965 or 1967 or 1968, I'd do it again. At that time, we simply had to get some people through the system who previously hadn't had the opportunity.

So as that rolled into the 1970s, it became increasingly clear that this kind of free flowing, idea of "You take anything; you know best; anyone can go into any class," was destructive.

At Miami-Dade, we began massive change in that as early as 1971 when we had what we called our first reform and at which we increased direction for people who weren't doing well, increased expectations, increased help. And I think it was necessary. In terms of a large institution, we were, without a doubt, the first to move in that direction. It took a lot of work to get there and a lot of time out, particularly as we moved in these directions, talking with people in the minority communities, to the leadership about what we were trying to do. The result was that we increased retention and increased completion, particularly among minority people.

Now, at the same time, most institutions did not make that move in the 1970s, and the result was growing failure. In other words, we admitted people, and I think we should admit people if they've completed high school, and then we did not help them gain the competencies they needed for proceeding into courses. We put them in places where they were doomed to fail. I think it took most institutions (and in California, it's taken until today), to move people away from thinking that any kind of "structure" is a barrier, when in fact, putting people in places or allowing them go to places where they were sure to fail was not in anybody's interest.

There is still this resistance to anything that limits what people can do, and it's a suspicion of minority people and actually it comes up more for African Americans than it does for other minority groups. But there's a suspicion that any kind of hurdle is a limitation and will stop people from achieving. And getting over the hurdle and getting people to understand that what you're trying to do is lift them to better opportunities is what the program is about. I don't think there's any place in the country where people have changed policy to go with mandatory placement...where that issue hasn't come up from some place, which is very often internal.

If students believe that what you're doing is punishment, particularly if you have mandatory testing in place, which I think is absolutely essential, and they've graduated from high school they think they're prepared. Students think they are being penalized by being put into developmental courses; you're not going to do well, and they're not going to do well.

One of the things that institutions overlook is getting across to students that this is going to help them. They're going to be more successful if they get this preparation and, secondly, that everyone who graduates from high school isn't necessarily prepared for college level work. But getting students to look at these courses in a positive, rather than a negative, way definitely impacts success and is something that is typically overlooked.

✑ Dana Britt Lundell

Dana directs the Center for Research on Developmental Education and Urban Literacy (CRDEUL) at the General College of the University of Minnesota. She is the author of numerous articles and coedits the CRDEUL monograph series.

For me, the term "remedial" still has an individual assumption about student learning. Many people are still saying, "Oh, you know, helping students, and we don't need individual students like that in our programs." That's that whole conversation that gets going. I think that it is still rooted in some of the semantics that we use. I think about the term itself and some of the politics surrounding what we do has probably influenced my thinking about the word. I guess I like the word "access" better. I don't know what that really means this early. When I think about developmental education, it does mean access and I think that helps me think about what I do.

When I think of the word, "access," and I don't know why that word always comes to mind, I like it. When I went to that European Access Network conference, they were using the word access as "access to education." It started to make some sense to me. When I was starting to think about access, I guess it's creating opportunities along the continuum instead of placing barriers to student learning and to a postsecondary education. It's sort of the opposite. It's providing... It's everything we do. It just sounds more positive. It's providing a support; it's creating institutional environments that are articulate about things like multicultural learning communities, or things that I see, like our dean puts in our mission—I think, "Hey! That's what access is: It's creating a whole institutional environment rather than just a single doorway for a single student to walk through," which, to me, is more developmental in terms of that connotation. It's the bigger picture. It's about the doors for the individual students, as well as the situations, and the climate and models of the institution that reflect... it's bigger... something on the systemic level too, as well as student learning. It's all a part of it. It's expanding the continuum of that. And this would include both undergraduate and graduate students.

For my dissertation, I interviewed dissertation writers in the humanities. I started off looking at grad students and how they were working with basic writers. I thought there were a lot of parallels. So, I started looking into the research and then realized there wasn't as much, or really a lot of stuff written for graduate students in graduate education. The same issues that we talk about in developmental education are there for graduate students as well. It's for the whole continuum including people going on the faculty track, new faculty. I see this whole developmental issue across the continuum. So, yeah, I think it definitely goes for graduate studies.

I think some of the same issues we talk about for undergrads are there along the continuum for grad students. I'd like my work to actually go across that continuum. I'd like to get back to some of my work on that because I see it connecting. It would be really interesting to be able to stretch the model a little bit, and I think that would actually do what we are trying to do, which is make this about all students and not just students in specific courses, specific programs and the kinds of things people want to do to shut us down and say that's just only part of the students.

⋙ Hunter R. Boylan

Hunter is the director of the National Center for Developmental Education at Appalachian State University. He has been the lead researcher in nationally recognized studies related to best practice for underprepared students. His latest book is What Works: Research-Based Best Practices in Developmental Education.

Developmental Education is a methodological approach that honors the whole student, the successor to remediation, because by and large, remediation didn't work. We moved to a different strategy, a more sophisticated strategy. So, developmental education refers to a series of methodologies for helping diverse and disadvantaged students. I see it as an umbrella term under which all activities designed to serve underprepared students fit. It refers to everything we do from counseling to advising to tutoring the developmental courses to assist our students. I prefer to call that coordinated effort "developmental education."

We rarely do a very good job of trying to figure out what students need. I get so frustrated with this debate over learning assistance versus developmental education. I really don't care much what we call it. I wouldn't have a major fight with some other name on principle. It's the concept that all of these services work together, organized in such a way that a student can access these services as needed, as that student's circumstances require and as that student's development requires. We encourage people to focus on the whole student and work hand in hand with people who are doing teaching in the classrooms. I rarely saw this in reality. I saw a disconnect between our verbiage and what was actually happening. I like "developmental" because, as I view it, it does what everybody was arguing should be done: Integrates cognitive development with affective development.

✒ Sharon Silverman

Sharon Silverman is the former Director of the Learning Assistance Center at Loyola University in Chicago and a 1999 Fulbright Scholar. She has co-authored two books, Learning and Development *and* Learning Assistance and Developmental Education.

The assumption underlying the term "developmental education" for me is that you take an individual where he or she is, and help them move at a pace that fits their ability, to move to the highest level they can achieve. But in higher education, it has a specific meaning: students who come into the higher education arena, less well prepared than others to succeed. So, even though we try to get rid of the stigma for "developmental," I still think there's that stigma attached to it no matter how you look at it because we're always talking about students who come in less well prepared. So how do you have a term "developmental" that means less well prepared and not have a stigma? I don't know. I still see it exists, continues to exist, so that's what it means to me. It means looking at the total student in a way that doesn't focus on deficits so much. That's what developmental means, not deficits so much but focuses on potential; that's what it means to me.

The terminology depends on where you are in higher education. Since I've been involved with developmental education, I think it's a positive that we don't use "remedial." I think the term that you use does convey a philosophy that you have about how you provide education. If you're using "remedial," you're seeing students with a deficit lens; if you're using "compensatory," it also has a deficit connotation in the sense that you're compensating. I think that the use of the terms does have an effect on higher education because it reflects your philosophy on how you view students. But "developmental" being the most positive of the three terms, it still has a stigma.

Whenever you're talking about any cohort that is coming in at a disadvantage, I don't know how language is going to help you make it a positive thing. Coming in less well prepared than someone else is not as good as coming in as well prepared as someone else, and that's just the reality of it.

✢ K. Patricia Cross

Pat Cross is professor emerita of Higher Education, at the University of California at Berkeley. She has authored ten books and over two-hundred articles and has lectured on American higher education in the United States and Europe. She is currently a trustee of the Carnegie Foundation for the Advancement of Teaching and the Berkeley Public Library.

Personally, I still subscribe to the concept of developmental education as connoting the fullest development of a broad range of talents; both "remedial" and "compensatory" imply "deficiencies."

In those days when I used the term "new students" in *Beyond the Open Door* I was primarily a statistician looking at demographic research. The term "new students" differentiated between students who scored in the top third of tests of academic achievement, very narrow range tests, and students who scored below average on traditional tests of academic achievement and were dramatically underrepresented in college. With the new attitudes about equal access and the advantages of diversity, those lower scoring students were beginning to enter college, especially community colleges. They were most likely a population of students "new" to higher education, and colleges and universities were not very well equipped to serve them. That's why I wrote *Beyond the Open Door*, to prepare two-year and four-year colleges for the onrush of "new students." Now, people have slurred over that original research definition to use the terms "new students" and "non-traditional students" interchangeably to refer to populations of students who have been consistently underrepresented in college populations. But in *Beyond the Open Door*, I had a very precise meaning in mind. I defined "new students" as those who scored in the lowest third on existing tests of "academic achievement."

CONCLUSION

This chapter reflects the common refrain that there is no disconnect between access and standards. What we have heard repeatedly in these stories is the need to look at the combined issues of access and support at a systemic level. Many of the interviewees discussed how institutions have begun reassessing their dropout and retention rates in an effort to increase their commitments to their respective populations.

Again and again, we heard that access and support cannot simply be addressed by open enrollment alone. Fortunately, there is a discernable trend toward looking at the student and the institution holistically while working together to create an environment that enables educators and institutions to keep their promises, embracing and supporting students and faculty across the institution.

The narratives in this chapter continue to frame the larger picture of access while leading us into chapter four, a discussion of institutional commitment and its role in laying a foundation for student success.

Chapter 4

Where Does the
Commitment Begin? ∂≈

As I've said, you cannot be successful, because of the nature of higher education institutions and academic faculty, unless the president is on board, up front in words and deeds. If not, it is going to be a low priority even though it should have a high one, and it won't be successful. (Robert McCabe)

INTRODUCTION

Most of the voices recorded in this chapter are those of administrators, faculty, and staff. They describe the effects of having, as well as not having, support from those individuals responsible for making significant decisions about the institution. This generally means that the president, members of governing boards, and sometimes state legislators must be committed to providing meaningful access. Bob McCabe, former president of one of the largest community college systems in the nation, talks about how he personally ensured the creation of an innovative program at Miami-Dade by going out into the community and building a base of support before bringing recommendations to his board. Robin Remich, manager of Instructional Support Services at a community college, speaks about the importance of having administrators who make the right hires and provide a model for a "good learning community." Mike Rose, author and professor at University of California, Los Angeles (UCLA), raises questions related to basic societal values as universities are becoming so "starstruck" that research initiatives are more rewarded than support systems for students.

Some of our storytellers talk about the philosophical distinctions between having the right to fail versus the opportunity to succeed. Juele Blankenburg, retired manager of Tutoring Services at Oakton Community College, relates that over the last ten years her administration has begun to view developmental education as a tool for preparing students to be successful even following their transfer to four-year institutions. Gail Platt, director of the Learning Center at South Plains College in Texas, tells us that back in 1979 the mantra at her school was that all students had the right to fail. She feels that the switch to an institutional philosophy of promoting the opportunity to succeed has been dramatic and that the president now speaks out strongly from this perspective.

Some of the stories told in this chapter indicate the lack of institutional commitment by describing the scarcity of resources and expectations directed toward students. Karen Patty-Graham, at Southern Illinois University, recounts how "bad" administrators at the university level often state that those instructors who work with underprepared students are "no more than glorified high school teachers." Too much of her time over the years has been spent on not only putting up with demeaning comments, but also in sharing successful student learning outcomes to prove again and again the worth of providing academic assistance.

Milton Spann, founding editor of the *Journal of Developmental Education*, reminds us that although it is important to have a commitment in the form of policy development coming from the top, it is equally significant to have it developed in collaboration with the grassroots educator. He also longs for the day when the concept of supporting students "rolled off the tongue of all decision makers" in a way that demonstrated their understanding of the necessity of helping all students realize their potential.

THE STORIES BEGIN

(We have kept the interview portions of the book informal, and, for the most part, have not adjusted the words to follow formal grammatical structure. Also in the interest of preserving a representative historical record, we have not altered either the language or contents of the stories to reflect our own views.)

◄ぞ K. Patricia Cross

Pat Cross is professor emerita of Higher Education, at the University of California at Berkeley. She has authored ten books and over two hundred articles and has lectured on American higher education in the United States and Europe. She is currently a Trustee of the Carnegie Foundation for the Advancement of Teaching and the Berkeley Public Library.

I was a visiting professor at Harvard, and I spent about six weeks on the Miami-Dade Community College campus studying community colleges and Miami-Dade in particular. Bob McCabe showed what could be done by a very strong and dedicated leader. I was interested in what he was able to accomplish at Miami-Dade. He managed to get people interested in new ways of thinking about education. He took it piece by piece, and introduced change problem by problem. I think that it showed me what a committed strong leader could actually accomplish with a huge, diverse, spread out, multicampus institution with new populations, new immigration, and so forth. It couldn't have been the easiest system in the world to deal with and probably one of the most difficult models in which to make progress.

✒ Robert McCabe

Bob was the president of Miami-Dade Community College in the 1980s. The school became a model, under his leadership, for innovating strategies that led to an increase in graduation rates. He advocated for the requirement of developmental coursework based on the results of mandatory placement tests for all first-time students. He also instituted a system of early advising where students were apprised of their strengths and weaknesses.

As I've said, you cannot be successful, because of the nature of higher education institutions and academic faculty, unless the president is on board, up front in words and deeds. If not, it's going to get a low priority even though it should have a high one, and it won't be successful. The other point is that your academic faculty has to be positive too. It's amazing to me how blind they are. I mean these are people who ask, "Why are they here?" "Why are we dealing with these kinds of people?" This is the sort of attitude that comes up when, in fact, what they should be seeing and what you should be getting across to them is, "Look what we're doing; we're being sure that the students who get to your classes are ready to take them."

I think first, the most important thing was recognizing we had a serious problem. I think the thing that was the turning point at Miami-Dade was the meeting at the medical center on campus. I remember hearing a faculty member say, "I don't want these kids measuring any dose of anything to give me," and a lot of heads were shaking up and down. I came out of that meeting deciding to ask a lot of questions. The answers across the board were that the volume, that the mix of people in classes, was getting so broad that the faculty could not be effective. Those ideas began to change the administration's thinking, and then they really took the time to study and to try and understand the context within which the college was working. They took the time to look at where they were going as a country, as a community in the future and to begin their work in that context. They took the time to come up with plans that made sense and took the time to implement those plans.

We developed a big package of things; that's a condensed description. I think maybe the two most important planks in the whole concept, well actually more help certainly was necessary and more intervention, were limiting classes and loads for people who were not doing well and not letting anyone proceed into courses for which they weren't prepared.

In our case here in Miami when we made the changes, I particularly went out and spent six months visiting with the community groups and particularly with the religious leadership and built that base before proceeding, before we moved anything, or announced anything, or went to my board with it. I think that was necessary. We built the base in our own college so that people would see that everyone can perform. So there are politics, inside and outside. Nothing is successfully implemented by people who don't believe in what you're doing or won't take ownership. In this society, you can't move programs counter to what the public believes in.

❧ David Arendale

David's perspective from the General College (GC) at the University of Minnesota provides us with an insider's view of what it is like to work with underprepared students at a research university. At the University of Minnesota, the GC has come under attack historically for admitting students who, many believe, don't really belong there. The GC faculty has developed a very successful model of integrating basic skills into traditional content courses to prepare students for an eventual transfer to the University of Minnesota or elsewhere. There is a constant struggle with the core faculty and administration to reconcile, providing both access and excellence. Access is considered by many at the university as having a deleterious effect on their attempt to become a more well-known research institution.

I also hear that we're polluting college by letting these underprepared students into the academy and somehow their presence makes everyone dumber or less academically capable. I don't understand that. College is about democratizing. I think that we need to have more people in college, not fewer, and they don't all have to go to the University of Minnesota. They could also be going to technical institutes. Frankly, some of the students I taught at the community college went off to make much more money at the end of their technical certificate programs than I'll ever make in higher education. So I'm not a snob when it comes to school. I just think that most people need some form of postsecondary education, and their presence within the academy doesn't impact anybody else.

Perhaps another misconception is that we are trying to change higher education from its original mission by including these students. As much as I've been able to review my history of higher education, we've always been concerned with taking students from where they are and helping them advance to achieve their goals. I'm concerned about any system that tries to prevent people from entering higher education. I'm concerned because they don't reflect reality.

In the 1960s and 1970s, whenever the baby boom started to ease off, colleges wanted to have more students in school and they sought various ways to do that. Admitting less-prepared students to school was one way. The other was, and this really saved many of the colleges, developmental education. Remedial education became a very high priority in the 1970s. If you are looking at community two-year colleges, or whatever the term (we use the term junior colleges), they see education as one of their major missions. The problem in education today is that the public four-year institutions are claiming that it is not part of their mission.

I find this deeply disturbing. I'm very much a kind of economic determinist, I suppose. I'm an oddity in higher education because I think there are three Republicans in higher education, and I'm one of the three. A colleague asked, "Why in the world are you in developmental education? Why aren't you an investment banker?" I looked at him and thought, "that's so stereotypical," but I just said, "Part of the reason is that if I want to have a retirement, I need to have lots of productive workers." I see a direct link between education and people being able to buy homes and vote in elections and participate in the arts and volunteer in their communities and to earn more and pay more taxes and be less likely to be on public assistance and such.

There's a growing consensus that we've ignored the average student too much. Higher education, at least in my lifetime, has focused a lot on the best and the least prepared. We have many honors programs, and we help send these students around the world on travel-abroad programs, to honors colloquiums, special courses, and such. We also have special courses for the developmental education students. But no one seems to do a lot for the average Joes and Lucindas and Laquishas who are in the middle. They get ignored and have high dropout rates as well. We must continue to reinvent ourselves and help institutions view us—developmental educators—as resources for change in terms of student retention, improved learning, assessment and accountability in programs.

Another major trend that I'm concerned about is the issue of limiting developmental education to certain types of institutions. I know it has occurred in some states, and I think developmental educators need to continue to show the relevance of our programs at all institutions, not just a few. I think about the words of Alexander Astin as he commented on the annual competitions for the best schools in the United States. He said that when you look at the analysis it's really about the quality of your entering student class: What are their ACT or SAT scores? What percentage of them are National Merit Scholars? And it's on the basis of some of these criteria that we make judgments of which schools are in the top 10 or 25. He goes on to say that we've made a major mistake in higher education. We have gone into the talent *identification* business by the way we define who can enter institutions. He goes on to say that the purpose of higher education should be to *develop* talent, in terms of how much change occurs between the time a student walks through the door of the institution and the time they walk out. He says that he gets concerned whenever politicians think that we need to segment schools so that they don't have overlapping missions. You know, we really ought to change the way we perceive higher education; we ought to be in the talent development business, not the talent identification business.

My spin on that is that if we really act on Astin's thoughts, I think we'll probably find some community colleges popping up in those top ten lists that the national magazines publish every year on institutional quality.

I get concerned whenever politicians think that we need to segment schools so that they don't have overlapping missions. In fact, I think one of the most techno-garbled statements is "mission clarification." That argument is often, "Well, we don't need to have developmental at a research one institution," or "You can just go to a community college or technical school," or "If the high schools would just do their job better, we wouldn't need all of this education at the postsecondary level."

Well, that's pretty naïve because whenever you look at the reasons why people select institutions, generally, the number one reason is that it's accessible in terms of geography. People don't have to drive 30, 40, or 100 miles to a community college to get their developmental education courses. They need school wherever they are, some place close and convenient. That's the reason why I think it's so essential that developmental education be offered at every type of institution. Now the form of developmental education may look different; here at the University of Minnesota we have a different model than I had at my previous college. But the issue is that you always need developmental education because you always have students who are not prepared. That's why you're going to need us everywhere; that's why people go to school. They need to have development in a variety of areas, and we're simply a part of that mission.

✲ Juele Blankenberg

Oakton Community College is an open-admissions college established in 1969. At least two-thirds of its students identify themselves as transfer students. It serves learners of various ages, cultural backgrounds, languages, and academic backgrounds. Juele told me a few years ago: "Once you help a student understand how to think about things and to understand how his or her own mind might work, it's just really amazing the differences that happen. We never look at a student as a fragmented piece. We try to see people who are whole. It is a gentle practice but of enormous significance." (Casazza & Silverman 1996, p. 153)

I'm one of the believers that developmental education means that I'm here to try to facilitate your moving from where you are to where you want to be. I think that can happen at any level of education, not just basic skills. We see evidence of that need all around. Certainly medical schools, graduate schools, all kinds of institutions are beginning to understand that the desire to achieve your own goal, your own excellence, is important.

At my particular institution, Oakton Community College, there is no developmental education department. There is the learning center, and developmental education consists of those courses that are college prep courses in the English and math departments. That's how it functions formally. In the learning center, it's interesting because we are really bimodal; we have kids who are stumbling and need our help to survive, and then we have the other end where we have kids who are going to get every single dollar's worth of education they can get. So, we work as much with students at the high end of the curriculum as we do at the low end, but somehow or other that C kid is absent. I don't know why we cannot intrigue them, but at the top and bottom we have a lot of folks. We do big business at Oakton. Last year, we had seventy-eight thousand student visits; we really do big business.

We've been here a long time, and the faculty trusts us. The kids, by word of mouth I guess, because we turn people over quickly in the community college, have come to trust us too. And we have a lot of people we're successful with; they get a good grade on that test, and they come back to share it with the learning center. So we build some community there.

There would have been a time when I would have been hesitant to say that the vision of the administration and that of the learning center were compatible. But, in the last ten years, there has been enormous evidence that the administration supports us well. They see developmental education, both in terms of basic skills and in terms of preparing students to be as successful as possible after transfer, as one of the functions of the college, and we fit right into that.

We have mandatory math and English assessment; English includes reading and writing. It's really placement, and it's mandatory. You can take 13 hours worth of classes before you have to take those tests, but you cannot go further than that. Cutoff scores and placement tests are chosen by the content area departments. Test results are usually delivered through a counselor. If not through a counselor, all the assessment results are delivered to Student Services, so I don't know if that means that they have a conversation, but they would have to go there to pick them up. We do have advisors within those content area departments that are there to talk to students. If, for instance, I were to be placed into Developmental Algebra, perhaps because I was using a computer for the first time and felt that was a disadvantage for me, I could go and talk to the math advisor.

Approximately 40 to 50 percent of our students are placed into developmental classes; that is really high. Placement is mandatory; you don't have a choice. Actually, we have this delightful policy that states that if you were placed into Developmental Reading, and you drop that course, you are dropped from all your classes. It sounds awful, doesn't it? But it is really wonderful. Student progress is followed by the Office of Research, and they are looking mostly at retention or reenrollment. We have shown pretty good success rates with this policy, and the success rate of students following successful completion of a developmental course is pretty good too.

Developmental here at Oakton Community College would be defined as preparatory. When I first started working here, probably 5 percent at most of the students were from outside the local district. Now, 24 percent of the population of students represents Speakers of Other Languages (ESL), international students, and minorities. As the demographics have changed, a lot has changed; you cannot believe it. The college has stratified all the ESL classes; we used to have just a couple and now we have about five levels. You really have to adjust what you are doing to fit the demographics. We try our best to address the needs of all incoming students. It's all kind of incremental and focuses on what we see that needs work. That's how our mandatory policy came into effect. Kids would sign up for Developmental Reading, drop it and then have difficulty with every other class. So the college said, "Well, let's fix that."

Interestingly, we suffer from the same situation that many community colleges do; our full-time faculty numbers are really pretty low and our adjunct faculty is really very large, but the adjuncts all have developmental training in their backgrounds. Right now, we're most concerned with our ESL population, but everybody who works with ESL students has some kind of ESL training.

I think that once we get past the point of believing in a "throw-away society," developmental education becomes really important. I see developmental education as enhancing our society as a whole, and that's why I think it's here to stay. I think that as the world gets more complex, and as the world becomes more credential-oriented, we become more estranged from one another and we're going to run on our credentials. I think developmental studies will be the basis of getting those credentials.

◄ᛇ Nancy Bornstein

Nancy is the director of the Learning Center at Alverno College, a liberal arts college for women nationally known for its innovative competency-based curriculum and system of assessment. She served as president of the National College Learning Center Association and was coeditor of The Learning Assistance Review.

Alverno College is a unique institution in today's world of higher education. It is a church-related, small, liberal arts college for women. It places a significant emphasis on providing learning assistance for women who often return to school after stopping out for years. From the president on down, assessment is at the core of this institution's mission and is used extensively to make decisions affecting resource allocation and curriculum.

I think broadly that developmental education is identifying, in terms of students, whatever levels they're at in the areas you are working with and helping them move to the next stage. We should be designing classes so that each class or each level helps ready that student for the next.

In terms of the field of practice we're in and the students who begin with our classes or begin with our services, our challenge is assisting those students to learn things that they haven't been able to learn before. Maybe it wasn't presented in a way in which they could access the information or materials, and we provide a way for them to key into that learning. Our department at Alverno College is not seen as an add-on; "Okay, we have these students who are not quite ready, so you take them." It's really seen as part of a sequential educational process. Not all students begin with us, but for the ones that do, it's a step that makes sense. As an example, we can look at the four communication classes in the college. They are all sequential, and students are placed in a course in the sequence based on results of their Communication Placement

Assessment. Students start with our Developmental Communication class, which is an integrated reading and writing class, and then move to the next communication class. All the courses are designed to dovetail each other. Students can also skip classes in the sequence; there's both flexibility and connection.

There is also an institutional commitment to students who begin with our program or use our services in various ways. It's a very strong commitment evidenced by the fact that we're funded primarily by hard money, not dependent on grants. I think this says something about an institution in terms of how it looks at academic-support programs and students in these programs.

I make sure our classes are responding to students' needs. That's not something a student sees directly, but that's what is going on. We make sure our classes and support services provide links to the academic demands in the advanced curriculum. We also design workshops and seminars to help students with professional testing requirements in nursing, education, and graduate work. I think that's a real contribution. I'm always looking for what needs to happen next. I think part of it is making sure, institutionally, that we are aware of students' needs.

Additionally, sometimes I work with students and have to say, "I don't think this is working." I've learned how to be honest in a sensitive way and talk with students about what's working, what's not working, and what options make sense for them. For some students, we question if a four-year degree is going to happen. When that happens, I'm not sure they think I'm all that great, but we work through their options and set up, partly in the school or outside, things they can look at as possibilities. Sometimes I arrange appointments with a career counselor, help them evaluate a technical college program, or do additional follow-up, so nobody is left hanging.

Placement in developmental courses is mandatory here if the Communication Placement Assessment determines a need for the course(s). I didn't think that was a good idea when I first came to Alverno; I thought, well, if a student doesn't want to take these courses, why should I force her to do this? But I have decided this is exactly the right way to do it. If we accept a student into the college, and we know she has deficiencies, say in writing, then we know she has to become proficient in writing in order to perform throughout the curriculum. To tell her she doesn't have to take that class is setting her up to fail. I strongly believe this at this point. To identify areas of weakness and then not to require that a student address those weaknesses just sets her up to fail and spend a lot of money. I've also seen that, even though some students think it's really unfair to be forced to take classes they feel they don't need, they soon see in most cases that they do need them. And they report feeling more confident and secure in later classes.

When a student is in a class where she and her teacher feel she needs some assistance, most often, the teacher and the student talk about that together and the teacher refers the student, using our referral process for a peer tutor. When the tutoring arrangement has been made, we send the faculty member a brief form indicating that tutoring has been arranged and identifying their tutor. And when the peer tutor and the student meet each week, a brief form is filled out identifying what was worked on and any questions. We keep a copy, and the original goes back to the faculty.

Instructors in our department provide teacher-based tutorials for students as well. These are set up on the basis of referrals from faculty, advisors, or the disability support coordinator. Referrals for instructor tutorials are made when faculty see significant issues that are beyond what a peer tutor can work with. And often that's not content; our instructors don't tutor content. The student is often struggling with core communication areas: writing, reading, analysis, or organization.

The college Disability Support coordinator also provides referrals. She will refer students for teacher-based assistance and for peer tutoring. She is somebody who sees students right at the beginning. When she is working with them, going over documentation, and talking about their past educational history, she may see right away that tutoring or mentoring is important, so she will set up that assistance immediately. This happens with our ESL students who also meet with our ESL coordinator to determine course and support needs.

We also have a variety of study groups that is established based on faculty requests because the course is difficult. We have a wide series of study groups. They're set up, monitored by students, advertised in classes, and students attend them on an as-needed basis. Study groups are particularly effective for weekend-college students whose classes meet every other week.

One other thing we've done to affect how the institution sees developmental education is to be involved in work across the college. We are all on college-wide committees, ability departments, curriculum committees, and faculty in-services; we are very careful not to marginalize ourselves. We are now seen as part of the academic fabric. I think this is true, in part, because people in our department are involved in adding to the curriculum and discourse at all levels, not just at beginning levels. That's where it is easy, I think, to kind of look back at us as somehow different because we work at the beginning of the curriculum. Really making sure that we are involved in all areas, at all levels, has had an impact on how people not only see us, but it also allows for our work to be seen as well.

We are also vocal about things we do; we inform the whole college when we redesign things or initiate a new program or investigate new education designs. That's kind of a model here. We design our classes to connect to the next classes, and we get stories back about how certain strategies work or how our students are the ones achieving new things.

I think that we have to be very careful not to disconnect with how the student functions in the rest of the institution. Of course that's critical because whatever we do with the students in our courses, they have to use those skills and strategies somewhere else. It's really important that we impact how courses are taught and how education is seen across the institution. Because education, teaching, and learning define our field, we may have thought and studied more about how students learn and how to teach than faculty who, through no fault of their own, never had a class on how to teach this population. I think we can't see ourselves as only serving the student. We have to see ourselves as having an impact on the student's entire education.

◄⟨ Hunter R. Boylan

Hunter is the director of the National Center for Developmental Education at Appalachian State University. He has been the lead researcher in nationally recognized studies related to best practice for underprepared students. His latest book is What Works: Research-Based Best Practices in Developmental Education. *Hunter tells of an incident back in the 1970s where one university president demonstrated the powerful effect across the institution of going out and personally connecting to students. He could have issued mandates from afar, but instead he went out and made sure the students knew he was, indeed, listening.*

It wasn't as if Temple University didn't buy into the concept of developmental education. Temple was a research institution; they didn't realize there *was* a concept called developmental education. I dealt with it by going to individuals and saying, "Here's how you can help this other individual" because a broader concept just wouldn't have played in that environment.

When I got back to Ohio in the 1970s, there was a great deal of student activism on behalf of the African Americans in Ohio and all over the country. The events at Kent State had an interesting effect on our institution (During a student protest against the Vietnam War, the National Guard was called to Kent State University, and several students were shot and killed.). We were all, of course, appalled by it, and we saw the riot that followed. My university was the only state university in Ohio that remained open after the incident at Kent State. They cancelled classes saying, "Stay on campus, and we're going to have open forums and discussions. We're going to provide a way for you to focus your concerns and anger and structure a way for you to deal with this."

That week the groups that were most vocal were the African American and Latino students. Our president listened. The Black student union presented a list of seven nonnegotiable demands. Rather than have any confrontation over it, he said, "These look reasonable. We'll have to assign some resources to it, reallocate some money and it may take a few years. Are you willing to work with us?" He just, you know, diffused them. He was good to his word though. He came back the next year and began shaking up the university to accommodate the fact that we were going to have more minority students. They would need more help, and we would have to do something about it. And it just so happened that was exactly where I was coming from; I got along quite well with this administration.

I remember being with some of the Black students when they were holding a rally. One of my students was talking to the provost's team. They were discussing the cost for accommodating these students. They figured it would cost nearly $5 million over a period of years. That student asked, "What did this building cost, Mr. Provost?" "Which one?" the provost replied. The student said, "This administration building here." The provost replied, "When it was built, it cost about $9 million." The student took out a lighter and flicked it on and said, "We'll look at it as a savings of $4 million."

◄₹ Gail Platt

Gail is the director of the Learning Center at South Plains College in Texas and has been actively involved nationally and particularly across the state of Texas in professional organizations. She has been at South Plains College for over twenty-four years. She has experienced both an administrative shift in perspective toward providing academic assistance programs as well as a legislative attempt to mandate statewide testing and access to college. South Plains serves a large Latino population for whom it is their first choice institution. About one-third of its students are not prepared for college work.

I came here to South Plains College in Texas, and I was in charge of a bilingual training program. It was a three-year program; I was hired in the second year and found things pretty much in a state of disarray. No one knew exactly what this program was supposed to be accomplishing; no one had a really good sense of what had happened in the first year. There was a lot of administrative and faculty support for us to develop academic support services for students through the bilingual program and to help those students whose first language was not English. So we started doing more assessment and trying to diagnose strengths and weaknesses and trying to develop special programs and services that would address students' needs.

Because of the strong administrative support and also the insistence of the faculty here at this college, we started a learning center. That started the second year I was here, and I was put in charge of that. I have been here for twenty-four years, and we have seen tremendous growth in our program. It started out with just four tutors; we also did the developmental instruction in reading, writing, and math. Now we have a large computer lab and fifty tutors a semester in addition to student employees in the lab. We do all kinds of seminars and short-term programs as well as regular developmental and collegiate instruction. And we also have a professional development component in our program that we provide for faculty at the college.

When I first came to South Plains College in 1979, we really talked a lot about the right to fail. That was our mantra—that students have the "right to fail." So let them come, and if they can't do it they will just flunk out. I think over the last twenty years, we have seen a total 180-degree turn. We don't talk about that anymore. Now we talk about the "opportunity to succeed." My argument during the earlier time was always that if a student didn't have the background, they were not choosing to fail. They were failing because they didn't see there was a choice. If they come and they take the collegiate curriculum for which they are not prepared, they will fail because they simply don't know what they need to be successful. When we put them into the appropriate programs, they can learn those skills and achieve those abilities. Then they can exercise their choice. Then they can choose to be successful. Here at our institution, we have seen a dramatic change. The switch from the right to fail to the opportunity to succeed has been very dramatic.

I know that our president today believes very strongly in the opportunity to succeed. He has talked quite frankly about how at one time there was this feeling that people had the right to fail. That is not his position. He encourages all the administration and faculty at our school to support the opportunity to succeed.

In Texas, the Texas Academic Skills Program (TASP) had a big impact because prior to 1989, when we started this statewide testing program, every school in Texas did its own testing. This meant that some schools did a very good job; they tried to assess students and place them appropriately. Some schools did absolutely nothing. Sometimes the larger the school was, the more bureaucratic red tape, the less they did to help individual students. Often everybody came in; they were thrown into one big pile. They were all told to take College Algebra and College Composition whether they had any background in math or English or whether they had experienced any success in those areas. So we had this persistent pattern of failing. It was only when the state got involved, and unfortunately it had to be fueled by the legislature, that change occurred. It would have been much better if institutions had gotten together and agreed to do something to provide a kind of uniformity and accountability. They could have done something collectively to show their responsibility to their students. But because institutions were not proactive, the legislature did it, and in some ways the legislature didn't get it right. So it has been full of compromises from the beginning, but at least it was a start at uniform testing that all institutions would use.

At open admissions schools in Texas, for example, at community colleges students don't have to take the ACT or SAT. Many times students decide the night before classes begin that they will come and register. So they walk in the first day, and the instructor has no information when advising the student about the student's preparation. It is simply a matter of opening the catalog and signing up for whatever was listed in that student's degree plan. I have seen so many transcripts where students would attempt to take College Algebra five or six times without making any progress toward acquiring any knowledge that would help them pass College Algebra. With the state testing requirements, we have seen real progress in that area; now at least we find out they have that deficiency in the beginning, and we put them in Beginning Algebra and try to help them through the progression to Intermediate Algebra and eventually, when they are ready, to College Algebra.

I heard so many college presidents when the TASP program first came into play. There was great speculation about the reading deficits among students. At first there was a lot of talk about how we are going to have to hire more reading teachers. College presidents, almost without exception, said "Oh that will be easy. We will just go and get some kindergarten teachers and let them do it." They had no idea that when you teach an adult sophisticated, critical, and analytical thinking skills that are necessary for college reading, it is quite different from teaching someone basic phonics in kindergarten. And there is this idea that anybody can teach developmental coursework. I think also that our accrediting agency, the Southern Association of Colleges, does not understand the level of expertise needed to teach these skills. I think our most gifted and talented faculty members are the ones who are successful in developmental education because they need to have a very broad background; they need to have a complete understanding, not only of their academic discipline, but also of cognitive development. The public doesn't really understand that; they don't have an appreciation for all the skill that is required.

The whole building across the street is going to be gutted and completely redone to be a teaching and technology center. We, the learning center faculty, are very excited to have classrooms, labs, and a faculty development center. It will also house all kinds of wonderful resources for students and faculty as well as the community at large. We have met with the architect, and we have had a consultant from Maricopa Community College, Dr. Richard Sheets. He came in last December and spent a couple of days on campus advising us and meeting with the architect. We have also had focus groups on campus. This represents a huge commitment from the top.

◀ᘓ Sonia Buckner

Sonia was a student at Alverno College in Milwaukee, Wisconsin.

Most of my instructors out there met my goals. Well, basically, Colleen, my advisor, sent notifications to each of my instructors every time I registered for class to let them know that these accommodations would likely be provided for me when I came in the classroom. But most of the instructors knew ahead of time and already had an overhead projector or knew my need to sit in front of the class or to have a tape recorder.

One thing I did want to see, maybe in the school newspaper, maybe have some articles on learning disabilities or more on what the academic instructional support service does. You know: what they can do; how they can help. And also let them know what types of students are attending the school. That would help bring it out in the open.

◀ᘓ Lola Romero

Lola received her GED after being out of school for thirty-seven years and currently works in the Radiology Department at a university medical center. She is currently enrolled in a BA program, and she is working toward a degree in radiology.

I think administration needs to be more tolerant of people going to school that are my age who have careers, like their hours. I understand that they run from 9:00 A.M. to 5:00 P.M., but they need to be more tolerant that people have lives besides those high school kids that come out and go straight to college. Their student enrollment includes a lot of people that work. Right now, especially during registration time, they have made a lot of improvements. Trust me. You can enroll online; you can pay by phone, and a lot of that is great. Sometimes, you have to go in and the lines are horrendous and they end at 5 P.M. So if you work a normal shift, you are not ever going to stand a chance and they may not be open on weekends. They have made improvements, but I think they need to keep in mind that the ages are different and that it's just not kids going to school anymore.

❧ Martha Maxwell

Martha is truly a pioneer in the field of student support. She received her BA in 1946 and her PhD in 1960, and has mentored thousands of professionals. She has authored multiple books and articles that are considered to be classics in the field. Maxwell provides firsthand insight into how university administrators tried to accommodate the first influx of students who arrived as an outcome of the GI Bill following World War II. She had no training in this area, and it was not expected that she might need such training. She also talks about how federal monies were first allocated to learning centers and the competing interests to obtain funding.

So lo and behold, I get called into the office of the president of American University. He said, "By the way, we need a reading program for our students; they are not reading well enough." And I said, "If we set up a reading program, what are we going to use for material?" He said, "Don't worry." And he leaned over and pulled a stack of communist *Daily Workers* from his shelves. He also had a machine that someone had sold him that had red and green flashing lights and a page slide that came down and covered the page to push you along faster as you read. So that was another introduction to reading . . . you had to tear the pages out of books for the machine to work. It was not a very functional piece of equipment. I found it better just to use the textbooks.

What happened was the government gave ex-GIs back-to-school benefits if they went to high school or college or took any kind of training after they got out of the service. I don't think they expected so many to take advantage of it, but it really altered some of our colleges. One of the things it did was to develop the counseling centers in large universities. They were veterans' counseling centers. And then of course, many of these returning GIs needed very basic help in reading and study skills. So they set up GI-based Reading and Study Skills programs in colleges, and that really is a part of what today has made learning centers one of the roots of that area. They got many of the same things we are providing to students today. They had tutoring, skills courses, and also lots of counseling. Maybe they even got a little better treatment than some of our developmental students today who are merely put into a course. At any rate, it paved the way for many students who had not really considered going to college, to achieve satisfactorily and to take part in the community in ways that they had probably never dreamed about doing before going into the service.

In the meantime, the learning center at the University of California at Berkeley started out as a reading and study skills center and a counseling center. Its reason for being was their realization that they were going to let more minorities in who would need more help. The way that worked was that they had money for the EOP (Equal Opportunity Program) that was matched 10 to 1 by the State Board of Regents to support the minority program institution-wide. Finally, the chancellor decided that was not the way to do it, and he said that each campus would finance the EOP program separately. By putting it under the campus, instead of getting all those matching funds, we were able to set up learning centers. That was not an easy thing to do because we had Chicano Studies, and they had their own ideas on tutors and tutoring. We put in for money and grants, and they would fight us. Then when we got the money, and grants would come in, they would say, "You owe us half the budget." So it was an eternal struggle, but by and large many students were helped and it became a large center.

✌ Jane Neuburger

Jane is the director of the Learning Resource Center at Syracuse University. She currently chairs the National Certification Council for the National Association for Developmental Education. Jane emphasizes the comprehensive nature for programs that span the university but emanate from the learning center.

At Syracuse University, I am directing a learning center, so I do the regular hiring and training of tutors. I work with difficult cases at the graduate and undergraduate levels, but by and large my tutors handle most everything. Basically, my job is to meet with faculty, staff, and deans of various departments to set things in motion. I give a presentation at new faculty orientation and for international teaching assistants each year. I've presented in a host of first-year seminars on learning styles, time management, and active reading strategies. I've had some very gratifying summer work with graduate students, mostly education students, who we hire for specialized programs, both a prefreshman Summer Start experience for students who take courses in the second session of summer term prior to enrolling in the fall and the Syracuse Success

Initiative, which targets undergraduates who wish to use the summer to advance their GPA or credits. I also have a graduate student in science education with whom I collaborate on training a learning specialist for the Women in Science and Engineering Community, a residential learning community. I'm beginning a collaboration with several professors and look forward to matching a model of learning assistance to their classroom needs.

I'm teaching a graduate/undergraduate pilot course on the pedagogy of peer tutoring and tutor training. This is an important element of the services through the Learning Resource Center as there are assistance programs all over the university. Part of my job is to connect with all of them, and I am continuing to do this.

You know, at Cazenovia College, in our learning center we saw between 50 percent and 70 percent of the entire student population. Granted, it was a very small college of one thousand students, but we saw a huge proportion of that student population because it was an accepted thing to do. It was pervasive. It was everywhere. I really think that's what developmental education/learning assistance can be: pervasive like that, supportive, in the classroom, outside the classroom. And that's where I think all of education ought to be moving.

What I mean by pervasive is, I think, we have to get into students' minds, some faculty's minds and administrators' minds that learning is something that happens not necessarily in isolation from other people. That's the message, that you're expected to go to study group; you're expected to have questions; you're expected to go to office hours and talk to your professor; you're expected to come to class having read the material and having questions . . . really work at getting the most you can from this education. I think that is what I mean by pervasive. I do not mean pervasive by forcing. I don't think it should be a mandated type of thing, but I think you make cooperation and collaboration an expectation and an accepted thing to do, seeking out assistance, working with others. We are all in this together. Faculty, students, tutors, administrators, learning assistance, and developmental education folks; we are all pursuing this great dream of education together. We should support each other, not make separate camps.

I would say my perspective has broadened to clearly understand that I need to listen carefully to my faculty colleagues and my administrators. I need to hear their thoughts and concerns and help them to make their cases the way they need to make their cases. It's really important to work with your deans, with your college presidents. Understand where they are coming from whether you agree or not. Go back and think through all that and say, "OK. I know that you are responsible to another body, the board of trustees." The deans are responsible to the president who has an agenda. The president is responsible to the board of trustees who has an agenda, and the trustees are responsible to the legislators who also have an agenda. So I need to understand that and continue to educate. We all need to know this; we all need to continually educate others, and we need to be adamantly steadfast that "our" students are "their" students as well.

I cannot believe that there's a dean or a college president anywhere who is not interested in student success. They need to hear both individual student stories and the numbers. Send out those success stories in memos, newsletters, and brag about your students. I think administrators also want to know the graduation rates and retention rates; knowing that, I must be prepared to meet with them to share those numbers.

We also need to buddy up with the statisticians of the world and our faculty. We need to buddy up with our colleagues who are required to publish or do it ourselves because we could do the research on teaching and learning. There's a whole movement afoot about not simply student outcomes but student learning outcomes. And I really think that developmental education has led the way for all colleges to think about student learning outcomes. Not only have we needed to demonstrate our value to the world, but also are definitely focused on the success of each student, one at a time. And those successes are not always captured in completion rates or graduation rates. I think we also have now an opening to say, "OK. Let's take a look at student learning. I know that this student has learned this amount of material regardless of the grade that this person has earned. How can we demonstrate such learning?" I know that accrediting agencies are interested in student learning. We know there are issues with grade inflation. We know there are issues with discrepant grades between this professor and that professor. So, how do I know that my student has learned what I consider to be important in whatever subject I am teaching? If it's reading, how can my students demonstrate that they can now process a passage, figure out what it says, and tell me what it says?

It's a lot of qualitative research, but I think we can lead the way. First of all, we are very close with our students. Secondly, when we have students who are struggling, we often work outside office hours or know the tutors to send them to. We are not the only faculty and staff to do this, but I'm pretty sure we see a large number of our students and are therefore in a position to be able to capture those students' insights if we work on it. The issue with assessment is always that people see it as an added-on activity. I think there is a lingering misperception that assessment is only about numbers. So if we can do case study research, you know, tell me about Jimmy, Samantha, and Sherone: What did they learn? Then we'll see the floodgates open.

I think we are in another cycle of tight money and tight budgets. I think that legislators, trustees, presidents, and deans are looking everywhere to save a buck. It's really just following the CEOs of the world, which I think is a shame. The students at Syracuse University pay for tutoring services unless their programs sponsor them. I'm giving away coupons for free tutoring this fall; otherwise, programs sponsor students for "x" amount of hours. The student comes in and signs in; it's based upon appointments only. They sign up, get a trained tutor, and they go off to work together. The paperwork gets turned in, and the tutor gets paid. There's a perception here that a lot of students can afford tutoring, but I know that there's a lot of students who can't afford it. When I have a student who comes in and can't afford tutoring, I have other pockets of different places on campus where I can send that student to get sponsored. It needs to get better than that. I'd like to change this by going to other departments who are offering academic support and say, "OK. Let's identify the issues campus wide, university wide, and see where we can go with this."

✐ Robin Remich

Robin has her master's degree in developmental studies and has worked in education for over twenty years. She is the manager of the Learning Center at Oakton Community College, Skokie campus. When Robin talks about mandating processes and being intrusive with student advising, she is letting us know that administration has taken a stand on these measures and is purposefully attending to the endorsement of policies for student success.

Oakton Community College has mandatory assessment. It's an interesting contrast because it's an open-access institution, so they don't really need any transcripts or anything to get in, just a high school degree. Everyone has to be assessed after the twelfth hour, so all new students are encouraged to be assessed, and they have to be assessed if they want to take an English or math class. For math they are placed anywhere from arithmetic, which is equivalent to 6th-grade math, through calculus. And for English, there's a cadre of ESL classes as well as developmental classes for native-speaking students.

The notice to take the assessments comes with the student's acceptance letter. They receive their score report from the student services office, but they are not required to sit down with anybody to go over their results, so they can just pick up their assessment report and sign up for classes if they want to. There is not a required advising piece to the process. Students can make an appointment with a student services counselor or advisor. There is not a separately trained person that sees just developmental students, so I would say that we are not very good at case managing. A lot of the advising at the community college takes place a couple of weeks before classes start, and it's mainly on a walk-in basis. Students are not guaranteed of seeing the same counselor they saw before unless they really intentionally have built a relationship with a counselor.

The students have a variety of reactions to the news that they need to take developmental courses. There's a lot of denial: They don't need that; they don't want it. On the other hand, there are students who realize they need it, especially I would say on the part of the more mature student, the returning woman who knows that she couldn't do math then and can't do it now. So, she just really needs to start where she needs to start. But the younger students, the more traditionally aged students, fight it.

Overall, there are academic progress requirements in place for everybody, but developmental students are not tracked separately. So at some point if they have been here for two semesters and have below a 2.0, they get a warning, and then they go to probation and then they go to suspension, but that's just the general academic progress standards for everyone. There are special programs in place that will do more close, what I call, management advising. For instance our program for students with disabilities will track them more closely. Our federal TRIO grant program tracks those students more closely, but the general student is not tracked individually.

The TRIO student retention rate is around 70 percent or higher. That program serves two hundred students a year, so they get what I call intrusive advising. I really believe in that. All their needs are being attended to. It's a one-stop-shop concept where there is an advisor who knows them and will call them and help them get financial aid, get them to career counseling, or get them to whatever institutional resource they need. So, I'm tending to believe in that type of comprehensive service where it's not just the academic support. It includes a lot of other needs, especially related to financial needs.

Most of the fulltime faculty is pretty good about providing assistance to students. In terms of knowing that they have small classes, they are very conscious of getting to know their students and their names, and also offering their help in office hours and that kind of thing. It breaks down a little bit with a lot of the adjunct teachers who aren't around as much. With those folks, they don't have the opportunity because they are not sitting in their offices waiting for students to come. We do have, however, an extensive tutoring service. We have typically eighty tutors or more a year. And those are peer tutors—who are students—who have gone through a peer tutoring course, professional tutors who are degreed people, and then some of the faculty tutor for us or volunteer their office hours to be served in our tutoring center.

I believe that administrators must hire the right people and build a community at the institution, a true learning community. They have to model a good learning community among staff and faculty, which is what we are trying to create for students. There need to be opportunities for dialogue and continued learning.

✒ Gladys Shaw

Gladys is the retired program director for Student Support Services at the University of Texas at El Paso. She has been very involved at the national level in setting standards of practice for academic support services in colleges and universities. Gladys provides us with her perspective on what drives administration to support learning assistance programs. It is not always the most altruistic motivation, but should that matter if their financial support and policies facilitate student achievement?

Creating access started in the mid-1960s with the antipoverty thing. And I think what stimulated it was federal money. I really do. I think institutions weren't too concerned until they saw the dollars. Now, being educators and supposing that we are supposed to have ethics and standards, we had to find some way to justify that. That sounds pretty cynical, but I really and truly think that had a lot to do with it. That may be my accounting background speaking. I don't know, but it seems to me that when the money was there, they went after it especially when the states quit funding them so well. I think some of the administrators who went after the money had a real desire to help the students. I do, but I think the institutions went along with it at first because it was money. But I think also that when they saw the success of these programs; I think that's what made it come around.

I think we've got two things going on now. We've got legislators and the general public that really don't seem to understand; they're cutting funds and things like that. But, at the same time, at least the institution that I'm in and the many people around that I've talked to, the institutions are recognizing the need to support these students. These students who come in as developmental students, they're here. So, I don't know that they're doing it because they believe in it, or they're doing it because they need to keep those students. And if that's what it takes, then that's fine with me as long as they keep them here. I think our president is committed, and I think some of the lower administrators are, and they have to do something. They have to follow her lead, I think, and so it's happening and I'm just delighted.

Our state, Texas, sort of mandated us to come up with a developmental education plan; that's how our University College came about. You know, they implemented the TASP test, a kind of literacy test, a rising junior test but they didn't call it that. So there's been a movement in the state to do that, but now they're pulling back funding. They've now said, "Well, we're not going to have the TASP, but we have something else." They've renamed it, so it's kind of a muddle right now. In Texas, I think more than any other state, the politicians have been involved in this. I think they've had one or two people in the legislature who were, you know, trying to address their constituency. You know the border area has always been a bone of contention in terms of educational funding and resources. So, it's been a long, hard struggle, and our president has gone a long way at getting us recognized for that. She's done it in different ways, and one of them is trying to serve the underserved population. She advocates for it; the tutoring and learning center was funded part by the state and part by the university. That was a line item, and she and her assistant were at legislative sessions lobbying for the resources.

We should be articulating with the high schools. We currently have a huge grant-funded initiative going on with the high school to prepare students for college, setting goals and determining what courses they need, that sort of thing. Our president is very committed to serving the population in the community. She is sending faculty to the high school to do workshops and professional development with the teachers. They took about five years and set up some basic goals related to courses students should take, and they seem to think it's being pretty successful.

We still have two study skills classes for those students with academic needs, mostly first-generation and low-income students. Our classes include one for critical reading and another for general study skills, and they are both noncredit. We always look at each student to see what it is they need, but most of them go through those two classes. We cluster those classes with an academic course so that we're combining study skills with actual academics so the students get the feel of how to really deal with the information.

◄؟ Santiago Silva

Santiago has been an officer in several professional associations related to working with underprepared students. He is currently a fellow in a national leadership program sponsored by the Hispanic Association for Colleges and Universities, which is designed to prepare individuals for leadership positions in higher education.

Santiago, an administrator for many years, talks about the need for everyone to respect nontraditional students and work together to ensure their success both academically and emotionally.

I was the vice president of Student Services and Development at South Texas Community College. Our division was made up of admissions and registration, counseling and advising, testing, outreach, special programs, judicial and veteran affairs, student activities, and financial aid. As vice president, I served on several committees at the college that afforded me the opportunity to continue working on developmental education issues. I worked very closely with the dean of Developmental

Studies on how we could assist students to succeed. We tried to incorporate as many student services with instruction as we could in order to better serve our students.

I think the term remedial has had more of a negative impact on our practice than either developmental or compensatory. When students are told they have to take remedial courses, they automatically identify them as "dummy" courses. They do not see the value of the course and how they will benefit in the long run from it. I think we are partly to blame for that feeling though. I think that a good number of our faculty in this field is in it for the job and not really to assist the student. Their attitude comes through in their teaching and contributes to the negative or "down" feeling the student has about these courses. I truly believe that it takes a very special person to be in the developmental education field, an individual who is truly passionate about teaching and learning in general. I hear many of our professionals say to students, "Take the developmental education courses, get them out of the way so you can take the real courses and get credit." With this kind of attitude, we start them off on the wrong foot. I don't think this attitude is widespread, but it exists and it hinders the process.

◄ Milton "Bunk" Spann

Milton Spann was the founder of the National Center for Developmental Education and the first editor of the Journal of Developmental Education. *Here, Bunk focuses on the need for decision makers to understand what a developmental approach to education really means.*

Well, I love the idea of developmental education and developing students, taking them where they are and helping them go where they want to go; achieve what they want to achieve and helping them accomplish their goals and objectives. I love that idea. I think, unfortunately, the term developmental education is a very difficult one for most people outside our profession to grasp and to own and to claim. I don't think we've made a lot of headway with state agencies, with legislators and other people who have a tremendous influence over the direction of education and particularly developmental education and equipping them with the knowledge they need to be an advocate for developmental education. They tend to make that a synonym for remediation. I think that many of these folks grew up with, and they seem to have a very difficult time breaking away from, the notion that all we're about is the remediation of academic-skill deficiencies. That deficit model seems to be so powerfully ingrained in these folks that it seems difficult for them to let it go and go to something that is reflective of what it is we really need to be doing if we're going to be successful. I would love the day when developmental education, or some term like that, simply rolled right off the tongue of all decision makers in ways that suggest they understand the holistic approach to education and the necessity of that for students to really realize their potential. But we tend, I think, to be in many ways more narrowly focused on skill development as the basis of education.

There was once a lovely little book written a number of years ago called *Islands of Innovation*. What caught my attention was the very title, *Islands of Innovation*. I think that's basically where we are today, islands of innovation. There are islands around the country in developmental education that are wonderful examples of what can be done to address the needs of students from a holistic perspective. But they are relatively few and far between; most of us are still stuck in that old model of education, remediating students and their skills deficiencies. I think we continue to do an awful lot of that drill and practice stuff. We have not really broken out of that mold to a large extent, yet those islands are out there. If we could bring better exposure to administrators and legislators and state systems of education that would encourage support and hold people accountable, we could be more effective. I am one who advocates the practice of the best we know about teaching and learning and holding people to high standards of accountability.

I think that the decision makers somehow have to become convinced that the kind of education we're discussing here is really the direction that we have to go in if we're truly going to reform and turn around the American education system. And until those decision makers, those people who fund this and who provide the resources and the policies that affect us, until they change their thinking, it's very difficult for us to get much past these islands of innovation that I'm talking about.

I wrote a piece a while back for the Education Commission of the States addressing this issue of policy decisions, and one of the things I said in that piece was that I think grassroots educators need to be active partners in helping develop policy that's going to affect their lives and their institutions. We tend to have policy coming down from somewhere above that is oftentimes written and developed by people who have a pretty great distance from the educational process. They come at educational policy from a rather bureaucratic perspective; the very folks who are going to be implementing such policy, if it gets implemented, are not included in the process. So, this idea of grassroots involvement in policy making strikes me as a very practical idea. I am not aware that there is that kind of grassroots movement, but I think until there is, policy makers are basically going to be making policies that have relatively little to do with the quality of the educational environment.

I look at the work that Arnold Mitchell has done with the TRIO program. He is a master politician; he knows how to communicate, lobby, and work with legislators over the long haul. All you have to do is look at the success he's had getting funding for TRIO and when other people are getting less money, TRIO is getting more money. When other areas of higher education are getting fewer resources to develop these areas, he's getting more money. I think we need to sit at Arnold's feet, consult with Arnold, talk with Arnold, do whatever we need to do to figure out how he does this and then work with him or establish an office in Washington.

John Gardner is a person who's had tremendous success with the *First Year Experience*. He is convinced that he's got to be actively working with decision makers like deans and presidents by providing workshops and producing documents that will influence the people who are at the level to make the decisions that are necessary to support the first-year experience. The *First Year Experience* is one of the most successful recent innovations in higher education, and it is growing by leaps and bounds in terms of programs offered at college campuses. I think that's exciting. There's a lot to learn from John and others about how we might break the mold. The perception that so many of our administrators still have, and legislators definitely have, is that we are only about remediation; that's what we do.

One of the things we try to do at the Kellogg Institute, which is held at Appalachian State University for a month every summer, is to try to influence the forty-five participants to go back and make a difference on their own campus, to stand tall and to be proud that they are in a profession that's worthy of standing tall and being proud; they need to believe that they are equals among equals and not second-class citizens as they are often considered at their institutions. If you teach remedial education, as it is often considered by administrators, then you must be somewhat retarded yourself; after all, it is not upper-division work and is not major coursework. And so I think sometimes administrators even tell faculty that developmental educators are second-class citizens because they don't teach upper-division courses. In my view, they teach the most important courses in the institution because they create the foundation on which all the rest of us build. When we do a good job of building that foundation, the students are able to make maximum use of the remainder of their education in ways that count. If you do not read right and you compute and think and problem solve and relate in ways that are not competent, then you remain handicapped for the rest of your life.

We have to claim that what we do is extremely important and own it, be proud of it and celebrate it. We've got to be willing to articulate the successes we have in working with students and to show people that we're producing the kind of outcomes that are equal to or superior to those produced in the old, traditional ways. We also have to recognize that we can easily be subverted by some kinds of successes, successes for example where we find ourselves with tenure and rank. With this comes much time put into meeting expectations that can lead us to being perpetuators of the traditional system. We have to connect with the tradition in order to gain respect, but at the same time we cannot get locked into repeating mistakes that were made in that tradition. That's an enormous challenge for us. We've got to find a way to move beyond it and be on the cutting edge of new thinking in the new century.

We need to maintain our integrity while getting inside the system and helping it move forward. We need to gain respect from our colleagues for the kinds of things we do with our students. I think it's an enormous challenge and certainly one that most innovators have to face no matter what area of education they are in. When they're innovators and they are outside the mainstream, there's a powerful force to kind of pull them back in and shake them up and make them look like everyone else. I'm concerned about that.

◆ೱ Karen Patty-Graham

Karen is the director of Instructional Services at Southern Illinois University. She has held many elected leadership positions in the field of developmental education at the national and state levels. Karen talks about the importance of administrative support and how she has struggled over the years to demonstrate to administrators how important it is to provide assistance to underprepared students.

We need to wiggle into lots of different opportunities in order to be recognized across our institutions. I think we need to find ways to get involved in committees. We find ways to interact with faculty members whether that means bringing faculty into our classrooms or whether it's going into theirs. Perhaps it's offering to provide some additional testing for them or offering to come in and talk about APA or MLA style. I think that as you build support with faculty, you also have to build support with your administrators. And those administrators can make a great deal of difference. I've worked with both very good ones and very bad ones. And working with the very bad ones is very frustrating.

The bad ones are those administrators who look on our students as dummies, who look and even refer to them in such terms. These administrators imply, and often overtly state, that our instructors are no more than glorified high school teachers. The same administrators don't provide support emotionally, intellectually, or financially for the program.

I have to continually prove that what we are doing is worthwhile. I develop a sort of a booklet at the end of each year that talks about our student successes because I know that if I can show that our students are successful in the university, there is no way that they can eliminate our students or program from the university. And I disseminate that information as widely as I can. I certainly have to play the game to the extent that I put up with demeaning comments, but I also find ways to provide reminders that if we weren't there a third to one-half of the freshman class wouldn't be here. If we weren't taking on those students, the faculty would have to be taking them on, and they weren't in a position to, nor did they care to, take them on. I have to constantly remind the administration that we are producing credit hours and that our students are successful when they go into English 101 and College Algebra despite their ACT scores and educational backgrounds.

I've been fortunate for the most part to work with people who have been very supportive, and that makes the job a whole lot easier when you can sit and talk with someone intellectually about what you're trying to do and why you're trying to do it and its significance. They show support then by making sure that your staff gets computers, the writing lab furniture gets replaced, and the staff gets professional development funds to attend conferences. Those are the things that demonstrate their support and make it easy to be supportive in return. In the one case you and your staff tend to be isolated, and you sort of circle the wagons. And in some ways it's sort of like you are against the rest of the world. It's nice to not be in that situation because then everybody in the department can sort of reach out and extend their expertise and their tentacles into other areas so that we are viewed as part of the university environment rather than a little isolated group that can be easily overlooked.

◄ David V. Taylor

David is the former dean of the General College at the University of Minnesota. While there, he promoted new initiatives and helped to develop a nationally recognized research base for the college. David was active professionally in the community surrounding the university and has led several research projects, investigating ways to support disadvantaged youth. He is currently the vice president of Academic Affairs at Morehouse University. David provides us with insights gleaned from his many years as an administrator and working with instructors to emphasize the importance of teaching and viewing students as partners in the educational process.

My work is in the General College at the University of Minnesota where I am the dean. When people from the outside look at what we do, they think it's a tremendous model and they understand the work we're engaged in and they know the odds under which we are laboring in order to produce the results that we have. But the university keeps asking us why we can't do more not realizing that we're about tapped out in terms of what we can possibly do with the structure and resources we're working with. It's never recognized as being good work. The institution continues to ask, "Can't you do something more in a quantitative sense that we can look at and pass back a value judgment on?" I find that tedious.

One of the things we have tried to do in the General College is to move away from the notion that the students who are in need of the resources we provide are tragically flawed and are in need of restorative work. We need to dispel thoughts that these people are inherently flawed and what we are about is to fill empty vessels with our knowledge. And we've always maintained that students who come to us have a lot of skills and lot of strengths that we can learn from. We need to see our relationship with students as a partnership where they are not necessarily looking for information we can impart; rather, we can introduce them to networks or realms to which they have not been exposed. If we can do this, we've gone a far measure in terms of being able to reach them, not have them look up to us in awe and aspiration. We need to be able to talk to students in ways that make the learning community a real community of people who are dedicated to the advancement of knowledge. That's what we are about in the General College, and that's the reason I am here. We have the largest portion of faculty in the university within our college who has received the university's highest, distinguished teaching award for undergraduate teachers. This puts us in a position to model what it is we are asking others to do.

Because we are a teaching and research institution, my faculty has to look like other faculty and engage in work that is valued by those who understand what a research institution is about, so our goal has been to be the best developmental education program in the nation. And that means not only taking students who are at risk and supporting them, but also doing the research on what are effective strategies for working with all students especially those with different learning styles. We do a lot of sponsored research on adaptive techniques and technologies for instruction; we do a lot of theorizing on best practice. The other neat thing we do is to look at the relationship between developmental education and multiculturalism or multicultural education. We see a direct relationship between theories and practices in multicultural education and their goal and our goals as an institution that watches access and excellence.

We have found out that a lot of what passes for developmental education work and remedial education work is practiced by community colleges. There are a lot of teachers, educators there who do very fine work and understand the field. They might be persons who are not doing primary research because that's not their field, but they're taking the research that's coming out and applying that to their constituencies. So, there's a natural synergy between what we do at the University of Minnesota and what is accomplished at Minnesota community colleges.

We hold joint meetings; we belong to the same professional organizations; we are exchanging information about effective ways in which to engage the populations that we work with because, often times, there is a similarity in the profile of students we are serving.

Our admissions office tends to be a little bit more selective; the community colleges are more open in their admissions. The need is the same when it comes down to effective learning strategies, for students of color, for returning students, for students with disabilities, the whole nine yards. Our articulation agreements accept students' two-year general education coursework in total, which is applied toward their four-year degree at Minnesota. We've skirted the issue of discrepancies in that we take on faith that the students are competent, and we believe in the credibility of the community college work. We accept their community college work without question; we do this because we are looking at ways to not impair student progress but to facilitate the transfer between the two institutions.

When you get into the business of testing again for competency and students get caught up in that, they waste more time, more financial aid. So, we've decided not to open that issue but to still facilitate the transfer. Now the larger question becomes whether or not students who transfer with an associate's degree graduate at the same rate as students who did not begin their work at a community college. And we are finding, on the one hand, that we are not experiencing a lot of students who take advantage of the articulation agreement. And secondly, students who do are not graduating at the same rate as students who would have begun at the general college and remained at the university for four years. They are just not completing their course of study.

Mike Rose

Mike holds a PhD in educational psychology and is on the faculty of the UCLA Graduate School of Education and Information Studies. He has authored numerous articles and books including Lives on the Boundary *and* Possible Lives, *which provide insights on the nontraditional student. Mike suggests that we must demonstrate the importance of good teaching and working with students who need additional assistance further by asserting that it actually gets at the core of our societal values.*

When developmental programs get threatened or cut or demeaned or whatever, I think that's more than just pulling the rug out from a particular cluster of people at a particular location. I think it perturbs really fundamental values. It is not just a question of institutional dynamics or of educational administration, it, in my mind, becomes a question of fundamental societal values. It is on a kind of personal, intimate level and tied to notions of individual development, of opportunity, of creating the kinds of institutional spaces for people to come at something; maybe to come at it again and maybe come at it yet again. It's about growing, mastering, becoming confident, and creating possibilities. But, hand in glove with that, there's a whole set of fundamental societal value questions I think that oscillate and resonate powerfully back and forth with whatever particular developmental program we are talking about.

All these types of programs and efforts seem to be threatened at least in many places, and the most current shape of a threat emerges around this whole budget business. The latest threat under these programs comes under the guise of budget cuts and budget constraints and institutions being squeezed and so programs get cut. That goes hand in glove with the fetish that we seem to have in higher education to continually amp up admissions requirements so that, at UCLA for example, the average grade point for entering students is 4.25. Now that's preposterous when you read the kind of work that's being done in the court through some of these civil rights efforts, like the Williams case in California. A lot of folks, some from UCLA, are suing the state because students have unequal opportunity to take the kinds of courses that even give you a GPA like that. So if you are at a poor school, there are very few courses, Advanced Placement, or honors that enable kids to rack up those kinds of GPAs. We have a star struckness for these particular measures of achievement and excellence like SAT scores and GPAs.

I don't see research universities like UCLA reversing their course in this desire to get kids entering the system that have these higher and higher and higher traditional measures of achievement. I don't see that changing. Because we are so star struck with these particular measures of excellence, and the very language that runs throughout these places; people talk all the time now about stars. They talk about academic stars. We've got the best molecular biologist; they recruited the best molecular biologist or the best Renaissance art historian or the best virologist, and he or she is a star. I mean even the language is a language that I find offensive. There is just this whole ethos of these particular measures of excellence. I mean, here is UCLA; it is sitting in what is probably the most culturally diverse city in the country along with New York. It has the potential of creating itself into the most extraordinary urban university of the twenty-first century. This would take visionary leadership, and it would also take bucking the kinds of trends I am talking about, but it would be possible, and it would be really exciting. But instead what we have is the application of two to three indices that people use to measure excellence in terms of both faculty and student recruitment. Unfortunately, that is bleeding its way down into the other segments of the educational system. So, for example, in the California State University system now there is a lot of pressure on faculty to publish more. And so what happens as that happens? Well, you know, faculty's time gets pulled in all these different directions. Maybe what would change them in the long term, since this is often what happens, is some kind of economic destabilization that causes institutions to recalibrate, rethink what they do and how they do it. I don't know, but I think it would take something on that kind of scale to change that. I think the state has an obligation to its citizens in a democracy, and that gets so eroded that the kinds of programs we care about are threatened.

CONCLUSION

This chapter reflects clearly a strong belief that there must be a philosophical commitment from the top in order to provide the support structure necessary to help students succeed. Most of the interviewees talked about their own institutions and how this philosophy was either embedded or not in the moral fiber of the school. They contended that this was usually a result of leadership that trickled down across all programs. The programs certainly did not always have a similar look, but they did promote collaborative efforts across units and committed resources to helping students. Sometimes they were more intrusive than others, but much of this has to do with the type of institution and its students' needs.

Several of the stories painted an even broader picture by talking about society's responsibility to providing opportunities for all students. They connected legislative initiatives including policies and budgets that allocated, or did not, resources to academic support programs. They also talked

Chapter 5

Building Support Systems: What Works and What Doesn't Work? 🙌

There are four or five basic human needs it appears all human beings have, regardless of culture, which drive your behavior. I tend to use that knowledge base to create an environment in which students are motivated to learn. I don't motivate them; I create the conditions. (Milton "Bunk" Spann)

INTRODUCTION

There is no dispute among those interviewed that comprehensive support systems are essential to student development and success, and that the delivery and type of support systems vary widely across institutions. Within this chapter, we hear educators; leaders and former developmental students talk about different ways of supporting students both academically and emotionally.

Santiago Silva urges educators to move beyond negative assumptions and look at the issue of affect and its impact on academic success. David Taylor urges educators to look at students in terms of the strengths they bring to the classroom. Both Robert McCabe and David Arendale describe what they call "Life Development," which goes beyond the classroom and stresses competencies that will help with life in general. Juele Blankenberg, Nancy Bornstein, and Jeanne Higbee look at the whole student, a more sophisticated, successful approach, they find, than traditional remediation. Martha Maxwell believes that students should not be segregated in developmental classes and that environments for learning should be carefully crafted to educate the students in ways of taking responsibility for their own learning. In addition, all the interviewees stressed that a strong foundation of trust is integral in motivating students not only to access available support systems, but also to continue using the institutions' resources to reach their goals.

It is also important to note that all interviewed expressed the view that support systems should not be created in a vacuum and that support must move beyond academic disciplines and become fully integrated into the culture of each individual institution. This is a holistic practice that helps all students, not just those in need of academic assistance. Through truly integrated support systems, students become immersed in a culture of academia and its expectations, and they are motivated to employ new skills and strategies in all of their content area coursework. How this happens differs from one institution to the other, but all contain essential components crucial to fostering student success.

THE STORIES BEGIN

(We have kept the interview portions of the book informal, and, for the most part, have not adjusted the words to follow formal grammatical structure. Also in the interest of preserving a representative historical record, we have not altered either the language or contents of the stories to reflect our own views.)

◅ *David V. Taylor*

David is the former dean of the General College at the University of Minnesota. While there, he promoted new initiatives and helped to develop a nationally recognized research base for the college. David was active professionally in the community surrounding the university and has led several research projects, investigating ways to support disadvantaged youth. He is currently the vice president of Academic Affairs at Morehouse University.

We look at developmental education as maybe a new name for an old practice in higher education, and that's where students acquire the skills, attitudes, and behaviors that are associated with success. I guess that is the definition used by the National Association for Developmental Education (NADE). You know, the field includes a wide variety of educational interventions and the professionals who deliver them:

services such as tutoring, extended orientation, some types of freshman seminars, study skills courses, supplemental instruction, counseling, remedial courses perhaps in reading and writing, mathematics. It's the types of intervention that are offered in a supportive, educational community designed to help students acquire those skills that are going to lead to mastery in higher education. We look at it differently from remedial courses.

Remedial courses seem to suggest that there is a body of information that students ought to have mastered, and haven't; therefore, we need to go back and reapply or make them work through these things to a level of satisfaction or competency. Developmental education doesn't do that; it assumes that students bring a certain amount of skills, strength, and we are trying to assess the weaknesses and work with them to master learning, critical thinking, and the application of those skills.

❧ Santiago Silva

Santiago has been an officer in several professional associations related to working with underprepared students. He is currently a fellow in a national leadership program sponsored by the Hispanic Association for Colleges and Universities, which is designed to prepare individuals for leadership positions in higher education.

I see developmental education as an opportunity for an individual who is academically deficient to improve and obtain their educational goals. It is a means with which an individual not only improves academically, but also personally. Feeling better about ourselves has an effect on our self-esteem. If a person feels positive about him/herself, he/she is going to be positive about a lot of other things. The self-esteem is strong, therefore having a ripple effect on other things in a person's life. The challenge that we as educators face is helping students see developmental education as something that is positive. The negative connotation it has is interpreted as, something is wrong with us. We are not up to standards. The negative connotation associated with developmental education keeps our students from seeing these courses as a good thing...they see them as "dummy" courses and as a way of keeping them down.

Assumptions underlying the term are negativism, weak, not knowing enough, an added step, not developed to its fullest, all negative assumptions when in reality in some cases it's a self-esteem issue . . . returning after being out of school . . . personal issues affecting academic performance. There could be many other reasons why a student needs developmental education courses other than an academic deficiency. I am amazed at how something that is so good for someone can be seen so negatively by so many. Sincerely, I think that developmental education is seen as something being wrong instead of something so beneficial. I have always worked hard at helping students see developmental education as an avenue that will help them reach their educational and career goals.

Nasrin Rahmani

Nasrin, originally from Iran, is a former developmental student who holds a BA from National-Louis University and is planning to start her graduate studies.

One of my earlier instructors was very positive, and that always affected me. In that classroom there was almost a paper every week, but it was her encouragement to say, "Oh, you're doing fine, you're doing fine." I started doing more and more and more, and then I felt that yes, I can do it. You know, it's all the attitude of how you're perceived, how . . . how you're nourished. I think that's very important, and a few of our instructors did that.

Students should take advantage of help. It's there and it's a mistake not to take advantage of such a great service. It's the first thing that students need to do to help themselves, to tell you the truth, because if they have a bad attitude, nobody can help them. I would suggest putting everything aside and getting help and . . . I guess it's just like a cycle. That once you start going to get help, then you feel better about yourself and then you do better. I got more interested and I was more confident and secure to do that. You know, it just goes on and on.

Of course everybody is different. And, I guess as a teacher, you probably have your own style. But, some teachers don't realize that it is very, very important for students to get motivated. In other words, they don't really motivate the students as much as they should. Probably, they should care more, encourage more. You know, motivation is different for each student . . . each group. And, I guess it comes from the experience of how you would approach. I guess because of my management experience years, I've learned that each worker, each employee, is encouraged differently. And, of course, the teachers see, or meet with, students once a week, yet they could really put a little more of their . . . I don't want to say they don't care, but more care, I should say. Asking students what they want in a loving, caring way, rather than just coming and going to the curriculum just like, this is it. You know, communicate more in a different level with the students. Many adults come in the evening, and they all have other responsibilities. They probably could be approached a little more differently.

Let's see, one of our classes was really communicating with people around you and to listen to them. That was the very important fact. That listening to them, it makes a difference. And when I practice it at work, it just shows me what a difference it makes to care enough to sit down and listen without interrupting people. And, I actually saw that example in our class. That everybody was trying to just talk and not listen to anybody and that was very frustrating for everybody. So, I took that as, ok, this is a really good thing to *not* do.

~ Robert McCabe

Bob is a senior fellow with the League for Innovation in the Community College and a former president of Miami-Dade Community College.

I think the term Developmental Education, is not, in my mind, particularly important. In fact, I think that people are using other terms that may be better. "Developmental" is certainly better than using remedial, because in many ways remedial doesn't describe the circumstance that caused people to be underprepared. But I think developmental is not inappropriate . . . it is beginning to acquire a negative connotation in the same way that remedial has. "Life development" is a term that I've seen around, and people are coming up with all kinds of other ideas. But the critical point is not the term; it is not having whatever the term appear in a negative context.

The study that I completed a year and a half ago showed, I think, clearly that people who complete developmental education, or rather who bring their competencies up to college entry level, are successful in life whether they take any more courses or not, or, whether they get any degrees or not. So, I think that the movement of someone from a position where they will not have good opportunities in life to a place where they will, whether it's additional school or whether it's going directly to work, is the positive thing . . . not about whether they took a course here and there. Many did not get degrees and then landed on their feet.

First of all, two-thirds of these people went to an occupational, rather than a track leading to four-year degrees, and I think we tend to deal with it as if everyone's going on to four-year degrees. The point is that the literacy or what I call the information competencies that people develop in developmental education courses are the very same skills that business and industry are looking for almost in every job. So that's a significant contribution. And even among those who got degrees, two out of three picked an occupational certificate or degree over a transfer degree. Here's the data, which you should collect, about how students do in those next courses after completing developmental coursework, and basically all the national data are positive about that.

✍ David Arendale

David is a former president of the National Association for Developmental Education and currently an associate professor at the General College in the University of Minnesota. His major discipline is history, and he has written numerous articles on access in the context of the history of higher education.

I understand the importance of working on the development of lifelong learning skills in any course. In grad school I used to think that it was the knowledge that was important, a body of knowledge that everyone had to obtain. I now better understand what I need to do as an educator: help students develop their lifelong learning skills.

Do students have the ability to pick up a book and read it effectively? Do they have the ability to think about multiple cultures, about how their culture reflects and relates to other people's culture? Do they have the ability to appreciate the best out of all cultures because we live in a multicultural world?

I think it's important to help students develop the kind of thinking and reading skills that will enable them to keep reinventing themselves as they keep changing jobs. You know the old adage was that most people change jobs seven times in their lifetime and probably have three different careers. So, it's the ability to process knowledge, and I think that part of this information age that we live in requires us to even have better skills to be able to discern the good stuff from the junk. That's part of the problem for many people: they're so bombarded with newspapers, television, and 24-hour news reports. Now, you watch news reports and they have those crawling ticker tapes with information running across the bottom. Some of them even have two of those ticker tapes running across; people are being bombarded with that and then end up turning on the Internet.

There are no sensors out there to help us identify what's good information and what's purely biased information. It makes it more difficult to be an informed citizen because there's so much information. So, I think it comes back to me, to what I'm doing in the classroom. As an instructor or a professor, I need to encourage students how to be able to manage their own learning environment. I think that that's very challenging today.

Though my adult students were very confident in some areas, their confidence deficit was: Can I really return to a classroom and make As and succeed? Also, they were dealing with multiple roles in their lives; they were full-time parents and probably worked full time while they were in my class.

Now I'm in a classroom with students with lots of energy, but no life experience. So, I need to be very careful in thinking about the culture of my students inside the classroom. In spite of their strengths, they might have been somewhat insecure about their academic skills and unsure how to navigate the educational environment. It isn't so much my responsibility to bring up the cultural differences, as it is to facilitate students' awareness of them.

(Note: It is important to mention that Minnesota has one of the largest Hmong communities in the United States. There has been ongoing friction between the Hmong people and the non-Hmong community in the recent past.)

Here at the General College we probably have about 40 percent students of color in our classroom. In Minnesota we have the largest populations of Hmong, Tibetans, and Somalis in the United States, and the three biggest ethnic cultural groups in my classroom would be Hmong, Somali, and African American. It's significant for me to value and reflect these groups because most of these students inside my classroom are going to remain in Minnesota. These communities, and many more that are emerging inside of Minnesota, need to be discussed, valued.

As I had a discussion with a student, I realized there's not very much about Hmong history generally reflected in those textbooks, so I need to find outside readers and outside reading to help talk about that.

It's important that I help reflect those cultures, along with European cultures, in our course lectures, and assignments. I want them to value things inside the classroom. It is very important to bring in relevant outside materials, and value minority cultures because often they're left out of the curriculum. Once again I've learned that education is not about me transmitting knowledge to students. That isn't the way it works. I näively thought that when I first started teaching history twenty years ago, I'd stand and lecture. The students would just close their eyes and absorb all of my knowledge. I still lapse into that from time to time, and I have to guard myself. It's so tempting to fall into your own habits and your own centrism. Ignorance, I think, is so often the source of many of our social problems.

Now I understand that I need to put together resources, and the classroom is a resource center of speakers, ideas and assignments, and carefully selected textbook readings. We have the World Wide Web, so we have a million web pages we can potentially select from. My role is to carefully present these resources and encourage students to pursue them. So, it isn't so much that I feel like I'm responsible because in the final analysis it's the student's responsibility to learn. It's not my responsibility to force them.

◄ɀ Juele Blankenberg

Juele, now retired, was the manager of Tutoring Services at Oakton Community College in Illinois. She frequently taught graduate courses in the field of developmental studies.

At the Learning Center at Oakton Community College, I can see a student holistically, and I can come from a student's point of view, rather than the informational broadcasting point of view that some faculty are tied to. That helps a lot when I'm in the classroom, because I think that you can be more sensitive to the individual, and you can construct the activities in that classroom, so that they are much more inclusive.

I, for instance, really believe in discovery, so I very often set people out on little activities that are going to give us some discovery learning. I believe a lot in collaboration, so I always try to construct teams, because I think that one of the things that we need to do is to be able to hear our voice saying our things, using our language, building those common understandings.

Maybe the gift that we give is to empower them. I would think that that's a good gift we give: we try our best to help students feel empowered, and to do some things about admiring their intellect to the point where they have an amenable intellect. That sounds corny, but it's really true. When you come into the learning center for tutoring, we do a learning profile. That's one of the things that we do that is really powerful. And that, for many students, is the first time they've had an educational conversation with anybody. Isn't that extraordinary? I'm always dumbfounded when they say: "Well, nobody's ever talked to me about my learning style, or how I study, or what my preferences are." I think that institutionally, that service is certainly a gift to students.

◄ Dawn Harrington

Dawn received a BA in English and would like to work in the field of journalism as an editor.

Academic support means someone sees that I have a weakness in an area, and they are going to help me overcome it, to recognize it, to find a strategy to help me to do better. I don't have a problem with that at all. Anything that will help me to do better, go for it. Now I go to a tutor.

I was fresh out of high school when I first came to National-Louis University. I don't think I took my education as seriously as I should have. But now, you know, I am much more grown, much more mature. I value tutors; I take advantage of them, when at first I didn't. I thought it was a violation to give me homework on my personal time when I was younger. And now I go home, I do my homework; I study and take education more seriously as a whole. I hate that it had to happen ten years later, but I am just glad it happened.

The Center for Academic Development is where I received the most help; they were very supportive. They were willing to extend a hand, and all I had to do was take it. But, that is the best thing I like. They had tutors for everything you can imagine, people to talk to; I just didn't take advantage of them.

Before I came to college, I was just reading. If you asked me what I was reading, if you asked me what I read, I couldn't tell you, I would just be recalling words, just actually reading with no connection to what I was reading. So, I remember one assignment. I was so excited that my instructor picked my assignment. She had us read articles each week, and the next week she would display what we had written. We had to summarize it. I still remember it now. There was a man in the hospital. I don't remember what brought him to the hospital. I think it was an accident. So I read the article and decided to draw a cartoon. I drew out everything, the man lying out with his leg up in the air in a sling. She picked my paper the next week to highlight. I said, "Oh, she picked mine!" She said this was really good; I displayed everything in the article with a cartoon. So I think with her teaching me to visualize what I read, I read more today because of that. I even joined a book club. I think she was definitely the best one, college-wise. What I like least about the support? I think it was all beneficial, I can't think of anything I didn't like.

Now I am an administrative assistant here at National-Louis University. I think it has helped me deal with people more, and it has boosted my self-confidence. I feel I can do anything anybody else can. I think that comes through with my job. I interact with faculty and staff and students, so I just feel I am 100 percent now.

I think the faculty met my needs, but I didn't know what my needs were. I was a bit too needy. I guess I was lacking something in high school, so when I got here I thought people should hold my hand through everything. It was sink or swim; I was drowning a little bit. They did meet my needs, and what I needed academically: where they saw problems and where I should improve. Yeah I think they met my needs.

I would tell students to see what the problem is or why they are experiencing difficulty. For me it was an excuse. I didn't do a paper because of this or that. With the excuse, I learned that it was just because you didn't want to do it. So I would tell them to really be serious. If you don't want to do college now, don't waste the financial aid like I did. Don't waste your time. Just go two or three years later when you are serious about it because it is not a joke; it is not a joke at all.

Well, I would definitely recommend the Center for Academic Development; I don't know if they still have the Strategies courses, but they were a big help. And if they are having difficulty in school period, I would say surround yourself with other students who are trying to meet those goals the same way you are.

I would tell the teachers here that college is different, but students still need that support from them. If you see that students aren't learning one way, try something different. They are not adept with trying to reach out to each student like high school and elementary teachers are taught. "No Child Left Behind" should be implemented in college, as well. Teachers should try to teach one way and if the class is still lagging and you still have half of the class not up to speed, then try to do something else to reach out to them.

❧ Lola Romero

Lola received her GED after being out of school for thirty-seven years and currently works in the Radiology Department at a university medical center. She is currently enrolled in a BA program, and is working toward a degree in radiology.

My psychology teacher is a forensic psychologist. She made the class absolutely fascinating. It was not about being a couch potato at all; she wanted us to learn about every kind of psychology so she made us do a lot of interesting research, and we learned. It opened up my world. It made me realize how out of touch I've been for years. You read the newspapers, and you listen to the news on television, but you just don't pay attention to it. You know what I mean? If it's not happening on your front porch, you don't pay attention to it. If it's not connected to your life that closely, you kind of push it aside.

For instance, Jeffrey Dahmer a serial killer, his mother lived right here in town, well, a little suburb right outside of Fresno. I knew that from when he was in the news and stuff. My teacher made us study Dahmer.

She showed us films of him in court, she made us look at him from a whole different perspective. I came out of the class with a different point of view. I actually found out what made him tick, a little. He didn't cut up those bodies just because he was hateful and he wanted to hurt people. He actually wanted to be close to them; he loved them.

My teacher hit home. She's very intuitive. There were sixty-eight students in that class. The first night she called roll, she talked to us a little bit and when she called my name I looked at her and said, "Here." We were in stadium-type seating in a huge hall. She looked up at me and said, "You've got a wonderful smile." She put us on a personal level.

Every week there we had key terms in our chapters. They were like a vocabulary thing. You typed them up and handed them in to her at the podium, and then she gave you your test. She spoke to you personally, and she knew every student by name.

One night she told us that a student had called in and said she couldn't come to class because she had a babysitting problem. The student ended up coming with her child. The teacher said, "Don't ever feel you can't come to class because you have a babysitting problem. You have sixty-eight sitters right here!" She showed a lot of films and if there was going to be something explicit she'd have the moms take the child next door to her secretary, and the secretary would give the child crayons and stuff to color.

When our teacher was lecturing, she welcomed questions; she wanted you to interact. That was a large part of our grade, how we interacted in the class. At the end of the class we had to turn in a five-page essay on us and how the class affected us, or what we learned from it, how we felt coming out of it. I was very proud of my paper and she liked it, too, and that made me feel very good.

I learned so much from that class. The book we used had just come out this year. She taught us all the real psychology stuff, the terms, all of that, but we did so much more, besides what was in the book.

◢ᶻ Martha Maxwell

Martha is truly a pioneer in the field of student support. She received her BA in 1946 and her PhD in 1960, and has mentored thousands of professionals. She has authored multiple books and articles that are considered to be classics in the field.

I am still working on this idea that students should not be segregated in developmental courses, that programs, like learning centers, ought to be open to any student. We have enough evidence, yet people still feel that underprepared students need to be sort of put off in a cave someplace. I do see some change in that though we still have a way to go. That is what I would like to see in the future. I think in general we are a little better at looking at realistic parts of what we are doing with the exception of the fact that a lot of people don't realize that developmental students have a hang up about being called "developmental" students. It's a pejorative term. It's not, particularly for the people that work with them. They should be happy that we are doing all these good things for them, but if they are rejecting the idea it's going to be darned hard to work with them. I go around on this at least once a year. Students who have taken a course and a third of them *saying* they were delighted to have taken it and a third of them *saying* it didn't matter. But that still doesn't get at the negative facts of being branded "developmental."

"Developmental" has so many negative connotations; it's been adopted by lots of different fields . . . it has become a synonym for "remedial." And that's what happens, and I wish that we could get rid of most of those terms we have inherited. "Learning assistance" still hasn't got contaminated I don't think.

I still think we have to learn to avoid compartmentalizing people, and stay open to the fact that they can improve. Not only do we need to give them a chance and support to improve but also really believe that they can. That gets conveyed, so it is sort of a belief or a hope that you have to have when you are working with students who show some hope, some brightness.

I think the thing that has changed the least is that there is still a big gap between high school and college for many students. The courses, the demands, and the expectations of college instructors are quite different from high school faculty. I don't think that students realize it, and I don't think high school faculties realize it. And I'm afraid a lot of developmental reading teachers don't realize it. What the reading students need in college is more than a general high school reading course they took before. It is not general reading; it is specific reading that you need to succeed in college. You need to be able to handle difficult academic material, and I think that it's costly and unnecessary to hire a specially trained teacher to work individually with college students. Much of what we need to do with developmental students is tutoring, mentoring, and demonstrating skills in the courses. It takes much better if a student is in a class, in sociology, and is learning how to read sociology than just reading whatever.

⮜ Nancy Bornstein

Nancy is the director of the Learning Center at Alverno College, a liberal arts college for women nationally known for its innovative competency-based curriculum and system of assessment. She served as president of the National College Learning Center Association and was coeditor of The Learning Assistance Review.

We work with critical thinking, analysis, problem solving, applying concepts, and metacognitive skills, things some of our students weren't asked to do before. So, indeed, these are areas where they start to see that our classes make sense and assist them to do college level work. An example is mathematics. Many students in our classes find this may be the content they struggle with. Particularly, I think, as a woman's college, we have a lot of students who struggle with the concept of math and the fear of math.

Our math classes are designed with strategies to address math anxiety built into the math curriculum. For our math and algebra classes, students begin by writing math autobiographies; we don't do numbers. We work from application; we start with situations. We start from so-called "real-life situations." We do have a textbook for practice, but we use a manual that the teachers have put together, which has articles, situations, data, and comparative resources.

A few years ago, there were a lot of articles about welfare and women who "cheat the system." There were also articles asking how a mother could live on such limited incomes. The students read both articles, then they would analyze each of them, and break them down, Ok, these stories are based on the same numbers, but there are really different conclusions. So, at that point they learned the math they needed to figure out the numbers and to analyze them. They backed into learning calculation skills, fractions, percents, ratios, or whatever. And, in doing that, they developed an understanding of how to work numbers and they could analyze what was being said. You know the old saying that numbers don't lie? Well, we really teach that numbers *can* lie. It depends on the presentation of information, and students must be able to question and analyze data.

We have lots of data in students' journals, talking about how differently they look at the world, how they analyze, and how they've learned to ask questions. This isn't a class where they merely memorize. It's something really different. And, students leave the course with confidence about working with numbers.

What we've been able to do, institutionally, is really exciting. About twelve years ago, our department instituted significant curricular changes in our math and language communication areas. In the communication area, we had a writing class and a reading class, and so on. It was what I would call a skills-based approach, and we decided it wasn't working. The research and our own experience confirmed that students weren't able to transfer isolated skills to their content courses. We decided we needed to teach communication in an integrated, content-based context. So, we redesigned our classes to be theme-focused and to teach integrated reading, writing, speaking, and listening. We also designed our assignments developmentally. So, from the beginning until the end of the semester, students are developing their ability to read, interpret, analyze, and respond.

The work we did was followed later by the changes in advanced communication classes. The college used to have separate classes and labs for reading and writing, and speaking and listening. Our department model informed the changes that were made in the college as a whole, so that there are now a series of integrated communication classes. The same was done with the math. Changes in our department informed things in other areas. It's interesting to think that the department that works with developmental students has had a profound impact on what has gone on in the rest of the college.

~ Sonia Buckner

Sonia is thirty-seven years old and recently graduated from Alverno College.

My most significant learning experience occurred when I was attending Alverno College. They not only taught me to recognize that I need to learn stuff in a different way; they also taught me different techniques for memory. I couldn't remember a lot of concepts well, so they taught me different strategies, like using flashcards, and provided me with a tutor to help me with my writing skills. They even suggested I carry a tape recorder to class, so I could listen in to the instructor a little bit more and refer back to it frequently. Those little ideas they gave me now help me at work. Those strategies actually helped me get my job and be successful at the work I do. They are applicable all the way through my life.

My greatest strength as a learner is, probably, I'm more of a visual person, and I can speak well on my feet. I kind of tended to shy away from doing presentations or anything, but I think they are highpoints for me now. I'm not having so many anxiety attacks, as I would call them. I am able to speak on my feet not only to one person but twenty people in the classroom. I could stand up there and tell my story.

I sought out academic support in college because I had found out that I have a learning disability. I got tested. That was great. I wish I been tested in grade school. They provided me with a tutor that I could work with, at academic support I should say. They lined me up with a tutor that helped me with a lot of courses that I was taking, and that tutor was really good to me. I found out I had a learning disability through college assessment. So, later on in life, straight on in college life is where I found out. They kind of started the ball rolling, and I started focusing and learning in life.

My experience with academic support was really good. Everyone there, the faculty, they didn't treat you like a stranger; they treated you more like a family member, which I loved. I had a great tutor named Colleen Barnett. She helped me to recognize things that I was doing; I was struggling with writing papers and spelling. She helped me break down why I write this way or grammar-wise, she made me focus more on the grammar terminology and taught me just to read my paper out loud while I proof it, not read it silently. She also helped me focus on catching my own errors so that I didn't have to use her like a crutch to help me focus or look for any errors that I made. They also had little support groups for other students who were like myself. They had like a small network going on. We all met, had "Brown Bag Lunch," they called it, for an hour. We conversed about how we were doing in class, letting them know how we were doing. I think Colleen Burnett was heading that program. She was good at that.

At first I was really embarrassed about it, 'cause I, you know, didn't understand it. And it was kind of like a shame that I had some type of disability or anything like that. Or, that I needed special time outside, with a tutor. But somehow they helped me to suppress that feeling about being embarrassed and stuff. They helped me realize that you shouldn't be embarrassed, or anything like that and understand that everybody learns in a different way. That made me start feeling comfortable and once I started getting comfortable with that, I was able to make assignments in my class focus more and complete those studies successfully. The academic support was an important part of the college experience, definitely.

I look at academic support as an additional tool. I just look at it as it's something there for you, no matter what your problem is; you can come and talk to anybody. But, it's just a way, or a tool that can support the students while they're attending college and usually beyond. You can always still go back for help once you graduate.

I did go to some of the support groups when they had them. But the tutoring kind of took up more of my time. Colleen had a group of ladies with the same learning disability, and we'd meet for an hour during the day, during school time, and talk about how our classes were going and shared new concepts, or strategies they developed for test-taking, or different study techniques. Those were the main parts I focused in on in support groups.

I'd rate the support along a ten, probably a nine. The bonding, the networking, the meeting folks, I think that was the best. And the way they made it possible and relaxed so that you could start talking and didn't feel shy or anything. They made you feel at ease.

Online support would have been great. I am able to access my computer from home and for me it definitely would have been more of a convenience sometimes. You know, to either have a chat room or something. It would have been nice.

I was in touch with most of the teachers, anyway. They don't do that anymore, but they used to highlight the issue and say, "I have a special person in my class," or something like that. It embarrassed the person, you know. You don't want to be marked in the class, getting all this attention. Kind of approach the issue as a whole, say something like, "everybody learns differently."

I'm a police officer now and I'm going to try to go to the business side; I'm looking into the real estate business now. Yeah. I'm using strategies now, too. The biggest one is the communication course, which I really hated; learning to negotiate, and analyze everything. And down to the writing, too, writing reports and stuff. I never really saw myself as a police officer, but opportunity knocked. I took the test a long time ago, actually. And my name came up on the list, and I went on in the academy. It was just the timing. I found myself going to school full time and working full time. I still don't know how I did it to this day. I used some of the strategies I learned at Alverno when I was in the academy, to learn some of those concepts, learn the laws and stuff. I couldn't figure out how to do that until I was getting tutored.

◄ᵌ Milton "Bunk" Spann

Spann served as the first director of the National Center for Developmental Education at Appalachian State University in North Carolina. He has over thirty years of experience in the field of developmental education.

My theological training was pivotal in my philosophical orientation to developmental education in this way: my theological training has a great deal to do with my understanding of the dignity and worth of human beings, of the high value that we place on human life, of the importance of the individual, of the holistic way of thinking about a person, not only cognitively and emotionally, but also spiritually. So, when I began to think about the roots of my own thinking about my approach to developmental education, it comes out of both the theological background and psychological background. My psychological background and my undergraduate work in human development were compatible with my theological training, and I think they reinforced each other. Insofar as I'm aware, I have not deviated from that way of thinking about working with students holistically in developmental education all of my career.

I think others share my philosophy, others in the field of developmental education, and I think there's a greater sensitivity both in the human development profession, as well as in developmental education, greater appreciation not only for the cognitive and emotional aspects of human development, but also for the spiritual nature of human beings. I hear more developmental educators sharing some appreciation for that aspect of human beings. I'm not speaking now about proselytizing to students in some religious way, but I was thinking now of respecting and understanding that they are spiritual beings, as well as psychological beings.

An example of what I mean by "spiritual beings" and how that interacts with learning in the classroom is, in part, a matter of perception because when I see my students, I try to see them through the eyes of spiritual beings and in each one I see spirituality emerging and developing. I have high respect for each of them in that way. Sometimes, I challenge them to answer the question, the question of "Who are you?" or "What are you?" and they will answer that often in psychological terms. Then I suggest to them that they might see themselves as holy children of the creation, and that they might think of themselves in lofty and magnificent ways, rather than little and unimportant ways. This, especially, is a primary responsibility of educators, developmental educators.

I think if developmental educators really care about whole person development, that they can't satisfy that dimension of human development and ignore it, and that they need to celebrate it and respect it. I try to do that in my relationship with my students.

We addressed the issue, in a very practical way, of whole person development. We not only were involved in teaching students basic skills, but also in working with them and helping them to realize their worth and dignity. As we applied the principles of reality counseling, we believed that ultimately, the person's responsible for his own behavior and that our job as teachers was to help the student recognize that responsibility, to support that student in coming to grips that he was responsible for his own behavior. We talked about the concept of challenge and support, and so what we were doing was challenging students to take responsibility for their own behavior, recognizing they were the only ones who could do it, and that we were there to support them as they took risks in order to be successful.

We even talked with them about some of the various sophisticated strategies that they used to fail and suggested to them that it would be the same strategies that they had applied to failing; those same strategies might be applied to succeeding. So we began to outline, in consultation with them, strategies for succeeding in the particular course work or perhaps in some life area that they were struggling with.

We found that the holistic community-oriented support that we provided for them in the context of their education was the kind of community of learners that really did help them come to grips with that irresponsible behavior that they had been exhibiting prior to arriving to the program.

Students who come to developmental education often engage in failure-oriented strategies such as: not asking questions, not taking notes, not showing up for class on a regular basis, being late for class, or not reading the assignment. All of those things are strong predictors of failure if you systematically engage in not doing those things. I think they are founded on fear; I think the student is afraid to be successful and spends a lot of energy often reinforcing those failure patterns.

I taught a course that I entitled Diplomatic Academics, and taught the students how to go about subverting faculty members into supporting their educational interests. And I told them such things as faculty loves, absolutely loves, students who ask questions. I would help them, for example, in other courses they were taking, to design some questions appropriate to the courses that they were actually taking to go and ask the professor one or two questions during the course they were attending and particularly right after class. I suggested that faculty members are particularly impressed with students who come as soon as class is over and say, "By the way professor Spann, I found what you said about such and such very interesting and I wonder..."

And of course this became a game; we called this a game and laughed about it and so forth. But when you get the students to start practicing these behaviors in the context of a game, they subvert themselves into being more successful because they get all this reinforcement from faculty. So that was a way of teaching responsibility.

I'm a big fan of the psychology of motivation. One of the things I believe that we find is that I cannot motivate a student; I cannot force him to do anything, but I *can* create an environment, which is likely to be motivational for him and the core, the key to that environment, is one in which there is a relationship between myself and the student, and between the student and fellow students.

If I can create an environment where these relationships are fostered, where there's greater trust and respect on the part of students for each other and for me as I'm engaged in a relationship with them, then that creates the conditions by which they may choose to be motivated, and often are. One of the keys to motivation is relationship. It's a fundamental principle, a fundamental need that all human beings have, and that's the need for a relationship. And so, in my classroom, I try to apply basic ideas we find in control theory psychology, which talks about basic human needs. There are four or five basic human needs it appears all human beings have, regardless of culture, which drive your behavior. I tend to use that knowledge base to create an environment in which students are motivated to learn. I don't motivate them; I create the conditions.

Well, this idea of "controlled expectancy" or "locus of control" again relates to these other elements, I think. When we talk about controlled expectancy, we talk about the extent to which the student or the person believes that they are in charge of their own destiny, the extent to which they believe that they can move the world and make things happen. To that extent, they're likely to be successful. To the extent that they believe that life is basically the result of luck, chance, faith, God, whatever it might be; that they're not really responsible, that great things just happen to you and you may be a lucky person and get good grades, marry the right person, and get a good job—then you really aren't at the core of making that happen. So, controlled expectancy was a variable in my dissertation research in which we discovered that students possessed what we call an "internal locus of control" that can be measured by several different scales. A student who has an internal locus of control is more likely to be successful in a developmental education program, and I would suggest at any other endeavor, than a student who possesses an external locus of control and believes that the external world is what really makes the difference. So again, we're back to the issue of responsibility, teaching responsibility and teaching students how to get control over their lives in a way that enables them to move the world and be successful.

I really think it's important that developmental educators get serious about creating environments for learning and all the elements that I've suggested and many others. Creating an environment in which we teach students how to take responsibility for their own behavior and teach them that they are really at the core of it that they themselves are at the core of their own success. It's not something that happens outside.

There's a principle that I also included, and it's a way of thinking called "choice." I think choice is one of the most powerful ideas in the universe, and when we really become convinced that we have a choice to make every moment of every day, asleep or awake, that influences how we live in the world. That's a powerful idea.

◄¿ Dana Britt Lundell

Dana directs the Center for Research on Developmental Education and Urban Literacy (CRDEUL) at the General College of the University of Minnesota. She is the author of numerous articles and coedits the CRDEUL monograph series.

Our campus hosted a conference by the provost's office for all first-year experience programs. General College was just one part of many programs that really think about freshman-year experience issues. I was thinking about the role of all of these colleges, in doing the kind of work that General College is doing overtly, about its own sort of research mission, and in terms of that continuum of access, in the various factors from student learning and student development to institutional climate. Those kinds of issues work for all of these programs, and I was just seeing that it's our job as developmental educators to educate all of higher education about this and somehow get our language and semantics to go in that other direction.

We have a lot to offer higher education, and somehow we need to package ourselves to say this. One place I was really clear about it was on my own campus. I guess we try to package it and make our case. It seems like that would be helpful from the vantage point of anything that's going on in developmental education has a positive practice for student access. Somehow, it's changing our vocabulary about it, but also getting the word out. I don't know how that works.

◄¿ Calvin Mackie

Calvin is an associate professor of mechanical engineering at Tulane University. He was awarded the Distinguished Alumnus Award from the National Association of Developmental Education in 2004.

They had reading labs and writing labs. So, I would seek out support whenever I wrote something, or when I was trying to write something and trying to get my thoughts together. I would go to the reading and writing lab and work with a tutor. It was great. The tutor was professional, supportive, positive, and upbeat. You know, sometimes when you go into these support systems, you look around and say, "Why do they have you here?" But, the people they had staffing these labs were very supportive. That was a very positive experience.

For me academic support is an ancillary organization, a person set up to assist and support students with things that they are trying to accomplish. Really I believe it's over and above that which we do in the classroom. It's not beneath it, but it's over and above. Not only have we taught you this, but now we've set up a whole network for you to go get the support to further learn this. I've had a dual experience because I was a tutor in the math lab, and was going to the writing lab for help with writing. As a mathematics student at Morehouse, I was a mathematics tutor. So, students used to come to me in a support organization to get tutoring. On one hand, at one hour of the day, I was actually helping students learn in math. And lo and behold, some of those same students were helping me in the writing lab. So, I was in no position to judge anybody because I was giving them what they needed, and they had a skill and talent such that 2 or 3 hours later, they were giving me what I needed.

That all made sense to me. There's no doubt about it. The fact that I was placed into this remedial reading class also humbled me to other people that needed assistance. I needed assistance in reading, and I had to seek it out. Other people were seeking help in mathematics, so to me, it was all the same. After I came out of that reading class, I was definitely reading at a faster rate, at a higher level. I had a greater working vocabulary. And, definitely, my confidence came up after I came out of the course.

I think confidence...if we really looked at many of our students, what's really killing them is their confidence. People talk about hardware and software, and I also say the "under-ware"—the things that are under the skin that are really killing a lot of our students. And it's confidence. Once my confidence got going, a whole lot of things really transformed for me.

◄ᴣ Jeanne L. Higbee

Jeanne is a professor and the faculty chair at the General College of the University of Minnesota. She has written numerous articles and monographs and is considered a national leader in conducting and advocating for research in the field of developmental education.

The students in the General College receive their academic support through their content area coursework, and we also have an academic resource center that has a writing lab and a math lab. The counselor advocate also provides some support. We have things like this first-year experience course. We're going to have a big lecture an hour a week, and a discussion section that meets for a 2-hour block at a separate time period. So, some of the stuff, like guest speakers and things, can occur in the lecture because we want to see if we can serve more students in a first-year experience course. That way the discussion sections are going to be taught by counselor advocates, and that will shift their work load a little bit, but that will also mean that there are some things...you know, when you're talking to students about the core curriculum, for example, you're repeating some of the same information to every student who walks through your door. It will cut out some of that because some of that can be handled in class, and when you actually meet with the actual student, the conversation can be more individualized. So, there will be some learning support. We will be addressing issues like academic anxiety in that class and there are some sections of that class in existence now, but relatively few students are served by it. So, we're looking at whether a couple of years down the road we might even consider having every single student who enters the doors of the General College involved in that class and how that will affect the workload of counselor advocates.

The assumption is that within each course, each faculty member takes on some responsibility for that learning support. And, then we do have support services. We have very specific support services like the student/parent help center for students who are parents; we have the Commanding English Program for students who are nonnative speakers of English, but we have the more generalized support services, too.

Here in Minneapolis, we have huge immigrant populations. When I first started coming here, all I was hearing about was the Hmong population. Now, if you walk the streets around the university area, and also out in the area where I live, it's obvious that the Somali population is growing in leaps and bounds here, too. So that's a whole different set of needs because you have students who were not educated in this country and have language barriers. You also have students whose educations were often put on hold for periods of years while they sat in various kinds of concentration camps or refugee camps or other situations where they were lucky if their most minimal needs, according to

Maslow's hierarchy, were being met. So, they are coming to both high school and college from just a completely different perspective. There have been immigrant students in different parts of this country forever. That's what this country is all about and one immigrant population doesn't necessarily have the same issues as another immigrant population, so you really have to deal with the students as individuals.

I'm not a lecturer. I was a counselor and someone who worked in student development, at first, so I tend to take a very student development orientation to everything that I do. I bore myself if I stand up in front of the class and try to lecture. The first time I taught that psychology course, when I first got here, I was filling in at the last minute for someone who burst his aorta. It was the week before classes were supposed to start so I had no preparation, had no idea when I came that I was going to be teaching the psychology course. I stood up there with overheads for about two weeks, and realized no, this was not going to work.

I tend to be very process-oriented in the classroom; I give students a lot of responsibility for their own learning. I'm not saying a lot of other people don't do that, too. But in some of the classes that I could teach very traditionally, I tend to ... I don't want to make it sound like I would teach the same way I would run a counseling group, but I think that I bring a lot of those perspectives to my teaching. Typically, one of the statements I get on my teaching evaluations is that I show that I really care about my students, and I think that comes from that student development.

I don't necessarily adopt some of the underlying assumptions that have been connected to the profession. I don't think the terms "remedial" and "developmental education" are interchangeable. I really hate the medical model, the deficit model for developmental education. I really do see it as ... I love Alexander Astin's way of looking at the Talent Development Model. I think of developmental education from Astin's Talent Development perspective, and that it doesn't matter where the student starts. What matters is how much the student grows.

My assumption is that the typical factors that are used to predict student achievement from an admissions perspective don't work for this population, and my own research supports that. You can't look at standardized test scores and high school GPA, or high school rank, and necessarily predict how the group that comes in under what is typically considered admissible to any given institution is going to perform. Some of the students that you predict to do well, are going to bomb. Some of the students you would predict to bomb are going to do well, so I don't like to make any assumptions up front. I have written a lot of articles that use terms like "underprepared" and "at-risk," and I don't even use those terms anymore. I tend to think of many students I work with now as underserved and coming from underserved populations.

I think preparation can take a lot of different forms, including having parents who know what's going on, or who are involved in their child's education. What a bonus that is as opposed to having parents who are completely uninvolved in a student's high school education or before or after. Sometimes parents do not know how to be involved. I really try to avoid making a lot of assumptions, and I think that a lot of what we do in developmental education that may be specifically designed for students who are considered underprepared is really just good teaching and would work well with any students.

✒ Mike Rose

Mike holds a PhD in educational psychology and is on the faculty of the UCLA Graduate School of Education and Information Studies. He has authored numerous articles and books including Lives on the Boundary *(1989) and* Possible Lives *(1995), which provide insights on the nontraditional student.*

What I can say in a very general way, and this is just from reading the newspapers and hearing things and my sense, is that all these types of programs and efforts seem to be threatened, at least in many places. And the most current shape of a threat emerges around this whole budget business. As the welfare state systematically has been rolled back and rolled back and rolled back, and then in the last two or three years there is, it seems to me, just attempts to take away whatever monies were available and giving that money back to people to spend individually, spending huge amounts of money on the war, other kinds of efforts. But, there's this systematic attempt, to really, as William Grider puts it, to roll it back to the McKinley era in terms of the state, and what the state's role is in some of the kinds of terms we're talking about.

I think these are fights that, as I said earlier, that go back to really fundamental value questions as well as saving your institutional skin.

This is not to say that a lot of programs that are quote unquote developmental or remedial or compensatory, whatever words you want to use, not to say that a lot of them are poorly done, or built on conceptions of students and their cognition and potential, that's really troubling. Absolutely not. And some of the folks in your preface, speak to that issue. So, I am not trying to, just out of self-interest, defend any and all efforts in developmental education, but I am saying that, in some fundamental way it's all fairly threatened right now.

Developmental education means the chance for somebody to grow, to develop, to extend a life; maybe to even shape somewhat of a new self. It also is tied up for me, intimately, in the way we think about . . . well, in where we think we live as a country. I can't separate that from any kind of core beliefs about what kind of society we think we are, who we ought to be, what principles we ought to live by, what guiding or shaping values should be at the core of who we are.

CONCLUSION

The stories in this chapter reinforce the need for a movement to acknowledge differences, cultures, learning styles, literacy skills, the ability to manage one's own learning environment, as well as develop lifelong learning skills. "Affect" was a concept that surfaced often; students claimed that increased confidence led them to push themselves to take more risks and try new strategies. Most of those interviewed stressed the need for enhancing critical thinking skills, strategies, and skill development to be integrated within content coursework.

Educators acknowledge that they must take charge of creating inclusive classrooms and curricula and the need to maintain high levels of expectation for their students. Administrators agree that a dialogue and partnerships need to be developed with high schools, colleges, and universities, and that multiple factors predict student success. Former developmental students insist that services such as intrusive advising, tutoring, extended orientation and supplemental instruction, and integrated coursework made a significant difference in their ability to persist and achieve.

These stories and multiple perspectives bring home the need for reevaluating the delivery and packaging of support, both academic and personal. Educators, administrators, and former developmental students

Chapter 6

Vision for the Future ❧

INTRODUCTION

What has repeatedly emerged throughout this oral history is that increasing access to higher education in the United States is not optional; rather, it is essential in order to prepare individuals to actively participate in society as vital and informed citizens. It also does not signal a decline in the standards of excellence and quality across our educational system. Instead, if access is implemented effectively, it contributes in a positive way to overall quality by increasing diversity and placing students at the center of the educational system. It shapes the system to meet the needs of the students rather than simply expecting all students to fit into a static system.

The policy of open admissions, while usually well intentioned, has often led to the segregation of students and created a stigma for those at risk of failure and in need of additional support. Institutions have historically looked at students with the idea of transforming them but have failed to look at themselves and how to effectively transform their own systems in order to better meet the needs of all students. We have seen through this oral history how individual educators and administrators have looked inward and learned from their students in order to facilitate their achievement. We have also learned of institutions that are moving toward a more systems-based approach; looking at the institution overall, its goals, and the way it makes access meaningful. Perhaps the most insightful stories, however, are those of the students themselves who shared how they felt once admitted to an institution: What has empowered them and what has had a negative effect on them.

There is little disagreement among those interviewed that providing access without developing a support system is meaningless. There is also little disagreement that access accompanied by a lowering of standards is unacceptable. We strongly believe that access and excellence can and must exist side by side, both for the sake of all students and for the sake of society. We also believe that the responsibility for this two-pronged approach must be shared—shared across levels of education, shared between instructor and student, shared among administrators and faculty—and also supported by society at large.

In this final chapter, we move from the earlier descriptions and syntheses of our oral history commentary to a set of five recommendations and related action steps for enhancing successful access to higher education. These recommendations have emerged primarily from our interviews and also from our professional experience and knowledge base. Where we thought it would provide a meaningful context for the reader, we have included citations from current literature.

Five Recommendations for Enhancing Access to Higher Education

Recommendation One: Provide Meaningful Access across All Types of Postsecondary Institutions

It has become a popular stance in recent years to contend that academic support systems belong only in two-year institutions and technical schools. Those who support this argument believe that students who enroll in four-year institutions should already be prepared and have little need for university-supported academic assistance. These proponents go on to say that by offering such assistance across the curriculum, the educational value of the institution is being diluted and standards are being lowered. This comes at the same time that university budgets are being slashed, and institutions are looking for ways to cut services. Even though less than 1 percent of the public higher education budget is spent for remedial education nationally, decreasing support for underprepared students frequently heads the list when it is accompanied by the rationale that it will help raise academic standards. The unfortunate result of limiting academic support systems to particular types of institutions is that it restricts access, limits choices, and often forces students to work toward goals set for them by others.

According to the Southern Regional Education Board (Abraham & Creech 2000), more than 60 percent of all remedial courses are delivered by two-year institutions and technical colleges. It also reports that since the mid-1980s, thirty states have proposed policies to limit remedial education to these types of institutions. Of these, seven states have actually passed laws reducing or eliminating the programs from four-year colleges and universities. Two of these states, Florida and South Carolina, have agreed that four-year institutions can contract with two-year colleges for remedial instruction. In South Carolina, the Commission on Higher Education determined that it costs more to offer courses in four-year institutions than in two-year institutions. In 1994, the commission adopted funding policies that prohibited any state funds for remedial education from going to the three research universities in the state and froze similar funding at four-year teaching institutions at the 1993/1994 rate. By delivering all remedial coursework at the two-year institutions, the state determined that it could save $1.73 million a year. By 1996, plans from all four-year institutions were submitted to the state, outlining their procedure for eliminating remedial education and entering into agreements with two-year schools to deliver any remedial coursework needed.

In a similar move in 1999, the Board of Trustees at the City University of New York (CUNY) voted to phase out remedial instruction from its four-year colleges and deny admission to students who were unable to pass assessment tests in reading, writing, and math. Those students would be offered opportunities to enroll in the system's junior colleges or take special courses in the summer to upgrade their basic skills. According to Traub (1994), CUNY historically had a reputation for being the "Harvard of the proletariat," and it provided the path to a higher education for many who otherwise could not afford it. Along with the move to eliminate remedial instruction, the board of trustees also raised the admission standards for the four-year colleges and forced many students, who may otherwise have chosen a four-year school, into the two-year schools. Studies by Lavin, Alba, and Silberstein (1981) found that students from New York City's two-year schools were 19 percent less likely to eventually earn a baccalaureate degree than those who began at the four-year institutions. These studies took into account students with similar high school averages who transferred from two-year schools. The researchers contended that the community college culture often discouraged students from moving on into senior colleges, thus denying access to the all-important four-year degree for many.

The National Association for Developmental Education (NADE 1998) responded to this trend of moving developmental education from four-year to two-year institutions. At its March 1, 1998, Executive Board meeting, it passed the following resolution: "Therefore, be it resolved that the National Association for Developmental Education supports strong developmental education programs at all postsecondary institutions regardless of institutional type or size." The resolution was based on the Board's belief that the restriction of developmental education to two-year colleges would, in effect, mandate students who needed this academic support enrolling in a community college no matter how inconvenient geographically it might be for them.

A very recent development, and one that is directly related to this oral history, is taking place at the University of Minnesota and its General College (GC), and is very representative of the tension created when access and excellence are considered incompatible. GC was founded in 1932 to provide a general education to a broad range of students. Its primary role has been to prepare students who do not meet the regular admissions requirements for the university. Its faculty and administration developed a cost-effective way to provide assistance to students by embedding skill development across content courses. In other words, students enrolled in GC not only learn core content, for example, history, math, and psychology, but strategies for learning are also taught and reinforced at the same time, within the course itself.

In the spring of 2005, the university president and provost supported a proposal to eliminate GC as a separate entity in order to promote academic excellence and to make the University of Minnesota a world-class university. GC would be absorbed by another college within the university, essentially eliminating its role of serving underprepared students. Also, since 40 percent of the university's freshmen of color are GC students compared to 17 percent overall at the university, this move could substantially decrease diversity across the university. Legislators at the state level support this move as they link it to budget issues and feel that students have other educational alternatives in the state system.

Taking another perspective, the Minneapolis City Council passed a resolution calling upon the university to retain the historic status of GC. The resolution reads:

> That the city of Minneapolis supports General College's efforts to maintain its collegiate status at the University of Minnesota and continue to contribute to the University's laudatory efforts to improve undergraduate education for the citizens of Minnesota, its commitment to access and

diversity, and its goal to become one of the top research universities in the nation (2005).

In a letter posted on the GC Web page (May 2, 2005), David Taylor, dean of the General College, states:

> It has been said that the state of Minnesota fulfills its responsibility to the underprepared, first-generation college attendees by maintaining a fine community college system. I commend the state for supporting an exceptional community college system but that fact does not exempt the University from its sharing that responsibility.

This is a perfect example of the ongoing tension between those who want to limit access because they see it as a barrier to excellence and those who favor the development of support systems to ensure that access is maintained along with support systems that facilitate success. (On June 10, 2005, the Minnesota Board of Regents approved the proposal to merge the GC with another unit at the University of Minnesota.)

The assumptions underlying the above arguments imply that community colleges, and preparatory colleges, like GC are of lesser quality and are intended for students who cannot succeed in a more traditional four-year setting. There are currently a few new wrinkles in this ongoing discussion. Today there are almost 1,200 community colleges in the United States, and in some areas they are reaching their capacity to serve. No longer are they focused simply on adults wanting to complete a technical certificate or pursue a vocational interest area. More and more high school graduates are choosing to begin their college education by first attending their local community college. Some students are finding it to be an affordable way to explore academic opportunities and discover a major area of interest before entering a more expensive four-year institution. Community college students are younger than in previous years with 42 percent being under the age of twenty-two years (Honawar 2005).

The structure of community colleges is also changing to accommodate this broader mission. In some states, community colleges are now offering a limited number of baccalaureate degrees. In Florida, the State Board of Community Colleges constructed a five-year strategic plan whereby community colleges could offer the four-year degree in areas of high need, for example, teaching and nursing. In other states (Washington and Arizona) seamless systems of education are being explored through initiatives labeled P-16 (preschool through the four-year degree) and P-20 (preschool through a graduate degree). Another rapidly growing format is the University College model, where community colleges invite four-year institutions to partner with them and offer the final two years of college on, or nearby, their campuses. This makes it easier for community college students who have completed their two-year associate's degree to finish their four-year degree.

According to a recent U.S. Department of Education report (Adelman 2005), community colleges are becoming a standard transition point between secondary and postsecondary education. Four-year colleges and universities are finding that their enrollment trends reflect increased numbers of transfer students who bring with them multiple transcripts from community colleges and other types of institutions. If institutions are "sharing" students and providing them with various pieces of their higher education that will eventually lead to one degree, it is logical to assume that there is an increased need to share the responsibility for learning outcomes.

Action Step: Construct a Support System That Works Within the Context of a Particular Institution and Its Students and Mission

Every educational institution needs to be very conscious of its purpose and mission and how that connects to the needs of the students it enrolls. If a community college states that its policy is one of open admissions, then it must take a realistic look at what that means in terms of supporting a broad range of students who enroll with a vast array of goals and academic preparation. On the other hand, if a residential, private, four-year college defines itself more specifically, it must look at the students it is recruiting and create a support system that will work for them. There is no one system that works across all institutions, and by simply acknowledging this, the issue of providing support becomes much less threatening and also less tied to a perceived lowering of standards.

Let's take a hypothetical example of a large community college serving a commuter population that is likely to be working while enrolled for coursework. We will assume that most of the students attend part-time due to their work schedules, but institutional data informs the college that for the majority of the students who come for a two-year degree, an intrusive system of academic support is necessary. Assessing all students for proficiency in basic skills becomes an overwhelming task, and a realistic system must be created in order for the assessment to be meaningful. At what point does this institution assess students? Does it block students from registering if they have not been assessed after enrolling for a specified number of credit hours? How are students informed of their assessment results? Will a letter informing them that they need additional assistance to strengthen their math skills be sufficient, or do they need to assign advisors to meet personally with students when they come in to register in order to counsel them on their options? What options exist for students once their skills have been evaluated? Will they be asked to take developmental coursework to strengthen their areas of weakness? Who will monitor their compliance? What are the consequences of not following the assessment advisement?

These are the very real questions confronting large institutions that enroll a broad range of students. Does the ethical and social commitment assumed by this type of institution outweigh the challenge of constructing a very complex, system–wide process of support?

Let us also consider the support system necessary to meet the needs of students at the small, selective, residential private institution. We can assume that the students attracted to this type of school have a more focused set of goals and that they form a more cohesive and probably homogeneous learning community in terms of their preparation. These students also need academic support, but it may take an entirely different form than the one at the larger commuter campus. They most likely all enter together in the fall term and could more easily be required to take a freshman year seminar or a series of courses designed to assess their skills and also be provided with a personal counselor who would know immediately if they were falling behind or having difficulty. The counselor would be a regular presence in the life of each student and would be able to customize a support system that might include tutoring in addition to coursework. The tutoring might even take place in the residence halls in the evening with a cohort of others who have similar needs and fewer competing interests than those of the community college student who is very likely working after class.

Does this more individualized, easier to monitor, system of support lower the standards of the small, private school, or does it ensure that each student receives the help they need to reach their potential and their goals? Does this ultimately raise the standards of the school because the English composition instructor knows that his students have access to an effective system of support, allowing him to push them further with their writing development? Couldn't the philosophy professor expect more critical thinking if it was a strategy built into the freshman seminar? Should this school lose the opportunity to help educate a future mathematician because she cannot write at the level necessary to succeed in her English composition class or think critically enough at first to compare and contrast different philosophers? Or should the school provide the assistance she needs to meet her goals?

Action Step: Create Academic Partnerships Across Different Types of Postsecondary Institutions

Let us take the same two examples and examine them from the perspective of creating academic partnerships. Suppose that a student who originally enrolled at the community college completes his two-year degree and wants to transfer to the private four-year school to finish his undergraduate education. How can the two institutions work together to ensure that his transfer is a seamless one? Perhaps they could collaborate to write an articulation agreement that would detail which courses in a particular area of study the student would need to take before leaving the community college and what types and levels of coursework to expect upon entering the four-year school. The four-year school would commit, through the agreement, to accept the student's credits from the two-year college. Essentially then, all he would need to complete his degree would be the remaining coursework.

While an excellent first step, an articulation agreement takes into consideration only the formal academic credits. What type of support system would this student need when entering this very different educational culture? Will the instructor expectations be the same? Will the student's critical thinking skills match those of the cohort who enrolled in the freshman year seminar? What needs to be in place for this transfer student?

These questions are being raised more often as transfer students become a common phenomenon across educational institutions. In order to enrich the transfer experience and not lower standards, institutions need to consider more dynamic partnerships. Articulation agreements are fine, but they do not aggressively reach out to the student before the transfer occurs. In light of the increasing numbers of transfer students, it makes more sense to encourage institutions to find ways of working together more actively and earlier in the students' educational careers. The four-year institution could offer some courses on the campus of the two-year college and team teach some of them with the community college faculty. This would help to ensure that the academic expectations, where they differ, would be clarified to both the faculty and the students and would make the transfer more seamless. Students could also be dually enrolled at both institutions to meet a similar goal of clarifying the expectations. In addition, the four-year institution could host a summer institute for a cohort of transfer students, to create a support group for them as they enter.

Whatever shape the dynamic partnership takes, it needs to ensure a level playing field for the transfer student entering a four-year institution. It is unfair to bring a student into a situation where the expectations are different, without aggressively offering support. This is almost setting the student up for failure before she is given an opportunity to succeed.

Action Step: Ensure That High Schools Raise Expectations for More Students to Pursue a Postsecondary Education

Rather than simply blaming high schools for mispreparing their students for higher education, educators need to work across the traditional grade-level boundaries. They should talk about a secondary core curriculum and competencies that are expected for more students. Traditionally, high schools have separated their "college-bound" students from others at the start by offering them a more rigorous set of courses. Often, this classification of "college-bound" is established prior to high school, is based on standardized tests, and leaves out the students who may not even know at that point that college could be an option for them. By the time they are ready to graduate, many of them have not acquired the basic competencies that will help them succeed in college, and they usually have not experienced a challenging curriculum. This is not due to a lack of talent; rather, it is due to a set of expectations imposed on them which assigns them to a less rigorous education. Perhaps college and high school educators could collaborate and think systemically in order to make those eight years more seamless and determine, together, what curricula could better prepare all students for college work. Maybe they could begin by recommending a set of competencies that all high school students should achieve before graduating. This, along with dual enrollment in high school/college, would go a long way toward setting expectations early and ensuring more meaningful access to greater numbers of students.

Using our earlier example of the community college and the four-year private institution, their faculty could create teams with the high school teachers. The teams could discuss expectations at both levels of higher education, their similarities and differences. They could actually work with students to help them think through their goals and begin to develop support systems in the high school that would start them on the path to higher education. An interesting model would be to work across all three systems and create paths for students that would offer choices based on their goals: from high school to community college to four-year college or from high school straight to the four-year college.

Recommendation Two: Programs Must Address the Whole Person

Due to open enrollment, past changes in immigration policy, financial aid and employment requirements, and competition for promotions and jobs, institutions are seeing an increasingly diverse student population. Baby boomers are working longer, often part-time in retirement, and may need retraining. Low-income adult students face multiple challenges while working toward a degree. Job markets are changing, and workers are returning to school in order to remain current in their fields and to gain additional credentials. More and more students are returning after an absence of many years, feeling the need for additional education to advance in their jobs or to change fields. Many students are single parents, new immigrants, and first-generation college students, who may be new to the culture and expectations of higher education. They must often cope with multiple responsibilities, working full-time or holding several part-time jobs and raising their families.

These new students are older, more culturally diverse, and in greater need of a combination of academic support services than those in the past. They may not have had a prior history of academic success. This new population often needs assistance with time management, negotiating financial aid, course schedules and child care, to name a few. Bandura (1977) states, "It is difficult to achieve much while fighting self-doubt" (117). Rather than asking for help, many become overwhelmed by these seemingly insurmountable demands and drop out in frustration.

Unfortunately, for institutions of higher learning, the characteristics and needs of incoming students are not always predictable. While most institutions provide academic support in one form or another, the philosophy and delivery behind that support varies greatly. This is not written as a negative statement. Who better than the institution itself to form a philosophy and determine delivery of a support system? Academic support and the philosophy behind it should reflect the needs of the students enrolled to best support that institution's respective population.

Problems arise, however, when institutions fail to look at their learning environments from a systemic standpoint. Many place their underprepared population into segregated, stand-alone coursework designed to remediate them. While well intentioned, these environments often lead to passive learning with little opportunities for employing strategies and skills they have learned. In the worst cases, students are tested and are then placed, with little explanation, into stand-alone academic support courses where they might practice newly learned skills in isolation. Stand-alone courses seldom address other factors that influence a student's performance, such as family obligations, and job responsibilities, nor do they address the student's personal and academic goals.

Unfortunately, students may not always be counseled as to why they must take what they perceive as "dummy" courses and are understandably resistant and unsure as to why they are barred from enrolling in "regular" courses in the first place. Without opportunities for prior discussion, students may perceive support courses as additional barriers to their goals. To make matters worse, in the view of the students, these stand-alone support courses often carry "no credit" or "institutional credit," and are accepted only toward graduation. If a student's employer is paying for classes, academic support courses are generally excluded and are categorized as not related to the job or degree.

It is not unusual for students who are placed into academic support courses to be underprepared in more than one area, and more often than not, they may be required to take as many as three or four academic support courses in succession. Not surprisingly, they become frustrated because they are unable to begin their major course of study immediately when their enthusiasm and desire are high.

Stand-alone academic support courses do not come without a price; they can add significantly to the cost of an underprepared student's college education. To briefly explain, there are three main types of aid. The first type comes in the form of grants, such as Pell and Federal Supplemental Educational Opportunity Grants (FSEOG) and may come from the government, state agencies, and individual colleges. Scholarships are usually awarded based on merit, need, family income, or other factors.

The second type comes in the form of work-study programs and is meant to help students pay for costs like books, supplies, and personal expenses. A federal program, work study gives a student access to part-time employment to meet his financial needs; the hours a student may work are limited.

The third kind of aid, low-interest, capped-rate federal loans, comes from the college or funds which can be utilized by trade schools, such as auto repair, cosmetology, massage therapy, to name a few, and are based on school certification. These loans are either need based or non-need based.

If students are required to enroll in numerous support courses, they may overspend their allotment of financial aid. They may then need additional monetary resources, which can contribute quickly to increased debt. The unhappy result is that allotments may be quickly spent before completing a degree program.

Action Step: Construct a System of Interventions That Address Changing Sociocultural Aspects of Incoming Students

So how do we maintain standards and deliver support while remaining sensitive to the needs of the underprepared student? There is much research to support the idea that skill enhancement alone will not make a "better" student; students need frequent opportunities to acquire the strategies, attitudes, and behaviors associated with student success and persistence. Svinicki (1991) emphasizes that the opportunity for the "transfer of learning to a new context is not automatic but results from exposure to multiple applications." The inability to enroll in content area coursework while being enrolled in academic support courses inhibits the opportunities students have to make connections to multiple learning situations and to employ strategies learned in support courses to a venue more meaningful, that is, content area coursework.

Institutions such as the General College (GC) at the University of Minnesota fall at the opposite end of the spectrum; GC offers two years of fully integrated, cross-curricular support—addressing student affect, fostering comprehension monitoring and self-reflection, as well as offering multiple opportunities for active, independent learning. Students are regularly mentored and counseled and their progress closely monitored by advisors.

Interviewees supported the concept that interventions need to be inclusive and ongoing. Additionally, these interventions must take into account the changing sociocultural aspects of these new students and must be offered in supportive environments designed to help students acquire strategies that lead to mastery in higher education. McCabe (2000) notes, "Minorities have made progress but are far from achieving educational equality" (34). Upward Bound, Bridge, START Programs, and University Seminars (often a theme-based core requirement for all students, transfer or otherwise) are several support systems that have been in existence for a number of years across the country.

The strengths of these programs lie in the close connections that students are able to make with faculty and staff throughout the length of the program. They also experience the demands and expectations of academic and social life on campus. This interdisciplinary approach to a course of study provides comprehensive instruction that is designed to enhance reading, writing, critical thinking, and time-management skills. Students are able to gain confidence and experience in academia within a sheltered, supportive environment.

Other interventions may include coursework enhanced with multiple opportunities for students to practice developing and transferring strategies and skills within an authentic, meaningful context. Interventions, when embedded in content area coursework, provide and support ongoing opportunities for *all* students to monitor comprehension, make personal connections, raise questions, and modify and transfer strategies and skills. Integrated coursework would also address the issue of using up financial aid allotments before the student has completed a degree program.

Action Step: Integrate Cognitive Development with Affective Development

In order to foster student success, it is necessary to look at the student as a whole person. Self-esteem has a strong effect on all aspects of life; Silverman and Casazza (2000) emphasize that "self-acceptance becomes equal to succeeding academically in a competitive environment" (p. 23). Self-efficacy is nurtured through contact with supportive individuals, and that support promotes learning and enhances motivation. This is where advisors can be particularly effective; knowing that someone has an active interest in your progress can be a powerful motivator. Silverman and Casazza further suggest that prior experiences and beliefs, expectations from one's social and cultural environments, and the learning environment itself play an important role in the learning process (p. 27). An environment that fosters a culture of support, and values the strengths that a diverse population brings to the institution, goes a long way toward removing the barriers, perceived or real. Bandura (1977, 1982) reminds us that what students believe to be true influences their motivation, actions, and affect, more than what is "objectively true."

Zimmerman (1990) offers a look into academic self-regulation and notes that students must have opportunities to develop and practice what they learn and that these self-regulatory skills also profoundly influence affect and motivation. Through self-regulation, students are then able to exert control over their environment.

Academic support must address social and motivational skills as well as cognitive ones. In addition, these systems need to find ways to foster self-directedness, adopt standards that are embedded in the student's core values, and provide opportunities for self-evaluation and metacognition (Bandura 1977; Zimmerman 1990).

Ideally, support systems should follow a model of strengths by valuing what the student brings to the academic table, tailoring support to the student's particular needs, and allowing for active, participative, and interactive processes that engage learners. Institutions must find ways to expand their academic support systems so that there is a variety of delivery options. Many more students are working either part-time or full-time while attending school and cannot utilize support services that are offered during hours that compete with their work schedules. To accommodate the needs of these students, support must change; hours in which academic support is offered must expand to include weekends and evenings. Delivery needs to be flexible, and services should incorporate multiple modes of delivery.

For example, it is becoming increasingly popular to deliver content area coursework in an online format. This means that students' class participation takes place online, and they usually do not meet with their instructor or classmates face-to-face. In this format, they communicate with the instructor and classmates via a "discussion board" where they are expected to read and respond to a teacher-initiated discussion. E-mail is often used in conjunction with an online course. While this particular format is excellent and appropriate for some students, it is not for everyone, but sometimes students do not have any choice.

To support an online environment, as an intervention for students experiencing difficulty processing course material or navigating the online format, one university's online or electronic classrooms now include a direct link to a staff member assigned specifically to help students in that course. To put a face on the support, the link is called "Ask Elke." When students need help, they do, indeed, ask Elke and she responds to each individual and often follows up with a phone call, an e-mail, or an appointment on campus.

In another instance, a faculty member had observed that his evening students were consistently having trouble with the research paper requirement for his course. When he suggested that students seek academic assistance, most demanded to know when he thought they would be able to do so since they had full-time jobs, family responsibilities, and were attending school full-time.

Working in partnership with academic support staff, a component of the course was redeveloped to make room for a learning specialist to work with students on citations, bibliographies, and what constitutes plagiarism. When necessary, strategic reading and test-taking strategies, and writing conventions were also discussed. This support was woven into the course content over the entire term with an emphasis on meeting course expectations. These are just some of the ways in which to support the "whole" student.

Action Step: Emphasize the Development of Strategies Rather than Skills

A fundamental goal of education is to equip students with self-regulatory capabilities that enable them to take charge of and monitor their own learning and to develop strategies that are essential to academic success; strategies are what enable students to determine how and when to use a skill or ability. Additional focus needs to be placed on opportunities for students to develop and refine their strategies and employ skills that enable them to exercise control over their individual learning. Perhaps it is time to reexamine class schedules to see that they allow for optimum learning time so that students are able to practice their comprehension monitoring and make adjustments; critical reading strategies, such as identifying overall patterns of organization/ texts; and visual literacy (looking at graphs, icons, illustrations, and charts). Metacognitive (thinking about one's own thinking) and information processing skills are needed for students to be able to identify what constitutes "important information," apply it to what they already know, organize it, and then make connections so that the information becomes meaningful to them.

To facilitate this process, institutions must rethink the delivery of core curricula. It may be time to create courses with an integrated, content-based context that offers frequent and ongoing opportunities to make connections and to transfer learning in an authentic, meaningful context. Most importantly, students must have multiple chances to monitor, evaluate, and regulate their own learning process in order to adjust their strategies and address problems in ways that specify goals and alternative routes to them, selecting appropriate strategies and applying them effectively to solve problems. This would allow students more than one venue to refine their abilities so they may be better able to synthesize and connect what they are learning throughout their education and beyond.

Action Step: Create Intrusive Advising Systems

As the population of diverse learners grows, so must an institution's support network, and intrusive advising systems must be created to enhance student success and persistence.

Not unexpectedly, all of the students interviewed for this text reported that the connections made with faculty and support services were integral to their success. Students liked knowing that someone cared for them, followed their progress, and offered an ear when needed.

Personal contact with faculty outside the classroom was another important factor in student retention and has a significant, positive effect on students' behavior and is also essential in the process of social and intellectual development.

With this in mind, it seems essential to create an institutional environment or learning community that is committed to fostering support so that students can manage their own learning environments and develop control over their own learning. If you think for a moment about all the information a student receives in the weeks and months prior to entering an institution, and again in the first few weeks of the term, it is not surprising that they sometimes forget the details of the services and support that is available to them. And, if that information is not something they need immediately, they may dismiss and forget it. When students do realize they need assistance, they may already be failing. This is where intrusive advising can make a significant difference in student persistence.

So what might intrusive advising look like? Intrusive advising works best when it is integrated and coordinated throughout an institution. McCabe (2000) recommends what he refers to as "ongoing student orientation." This repeated exposure to services and opportunities can increase expectations, educate students as to why they are in need of support, and remind them what that support will look like. These support systems must take into account multiple methodologies for a diverse and underprepared population and must also include faculty from all disciplines and library staff, as well as representatives from student services and financial aid.

A system of support that includes a focus on increased contact with and direction for the underprepared student, goal setting, and an action plan, will reinforce strategies for best using that support. Additionally, this system of interconnected support integrates academic programs with institutional and community services in a way that is holistic and connected with the communities from which the institutions' population is derived. Support provided within the context of a student's whole education fosters ongoing opportunities for success, high expectations for students and the institution rather than creating barriers.

Action Step: Monitor Progress of Developmental Students
across a Longer Period of Time

In order for an institution to gauge what interventions are effective, the student persistence rates need to be closely monitored over an extended period of time. Underprepared students often stop out and start again several times before they complete their degrees. Students may also leave a four-year institution, and complete their two-year degree at a community college. Having all this information is essential for creating institutional interventions that are appropriate to the particular needs of a diverse population, so data collection becomes integral to the process.

Appropriate data need to be collected on many levels throughout the institution. Access to this information may mean long-term planning, collaboration, and coordination among departments in order to monitor the progress of individual students, or cohorts; it may mean collecting examples of academic performance or using the same assessment instruments across multiple terms. The idea is to track student progress toward intended goals in order to improve the caliber and delivery of institutional support.

Recommendation Three: Integrate Support Systems in a Meaningful Way Across the Institution

In order to be meaningful and really make a difference to the levels of student persistence and achievement, any system of support must be embedded into the culture of the institution. That is why it must be developed with the particular needs of the institution in mind. One size definitely does not fit all. If a support system is set aside and managed by individuals who are treated differently and who do not work side by side with core programs, it simply will not be effective. If it is supported only by external funds, for example, federal monies or state grants, it will not be accepted as an integral part of the school's purpose. It actually needs to be reflected, in some fashion, in the mission or core values of the institution. By doing this, there is ownership across the institution, and there will be an expectation that all units demonstrate how they link to this overall value system of the college.

Frequently, systems of academic support rely on external funding and are accountable only to their funding agent, often the federal government, who may have a different agenda than that of the institution. It is looking at large cohorts of students and most often measures success through a quantitative lens, for example, number of students served or the range of diverse cultural backgrounds or scores on a standardized test. While these measures constitute a component of academic support, they are not really informing the institution about how to strategically plan for improved student persistence rates or how the students perform once they complete the requirements of the grant and need to achieve in core areas of study. When support programs are built into the basic budget of the institution, they become accountable in a way that is tied more directly to its mission.

Some institutions have academic departments, led by core faculty, that deliver coursework specifically designed to meet the needs of incoming students who are not completely prepared to meet all the standards for success at the institution. These departments work closely with faculty across the curriculum to determine which students are not ready to enroll in certain core courses and which academic strategies need to be taught to ensure student success upon completion of the preparatory course. For instance, a basic writing course delivered through such a department would be developed by both the basic skills faculty and the English Department. The department delivering the basic skills coursework is held accountable, as is the English Department, for student outcomes and success in subsequent writing courses and overall persistence at the institution. The faculty in each department works together collegially and assumes responsibility for student success. Both faculties together determine which students enter the preparatory courses and when they are ready to move into the core courses.

In another institution where the support system is based entirely on a federal grant and is limited to a population of students determined by the criteria of the grant, it is often managed by staff that has little communication with core faculty. The staff is held accountable to external standards set up by the funding agency, which are not always reflective of those embedded in the core curriculum. In fact, the expectations are often lower than those of the institution, and the outcomes are not measured by success in subsequent courses. The outcomes data are judged by the external agency and not the core faculty, thus keeping the support system off to the side.

Action Step: Create a System of Shared Decision Making Across Units

The organization described above with academic departments dedicated to preparing students for success across the curriculum is one way to ensure that the system of support will be shared across units. The faculty, in this type of structure, works together to make decisions regarding initial assessment of incoming students and what the cutoff point is for those needing additional support. They determine what assessment instruments to use that are compatible with institutional goals. For instance, if students are required to write intensively across all coursework in order to succeed, the faculty may decide to require an essay for all incoming students that will be evaluated by a team made up of instructors from across the curriculum.

They may develop a rubric together that reflects the criteria necessary for success across the curriculum. Based on the initial assessment, students will be advised to either take a preparatory course or immediately enter a core course. This then brings another unit into the process: advisors. The advisors will communicate to students the results of the placement exams and explain the implications. They become an important part of the equation as students rely on them to clarify any confusion and lower their anxiety level. In order for this to work, the advisors need to work closely with the faculty to understand the nuances of the whole process.

The reason that such a department exists expressly to deliver preparatory coursework goes back to the institutional mission and purpose. There would not be such a unit if the institution did not believe in the basic value of embedding a system of support into its culture. By creating a department devoted to this purpose and hiring faculty with this expertise, the institution puts it on the same level with other departments and curricula and demonstrates its overall commitment to supporting students.

Action Step: Decrease Dependence on External Funding Sources

While many institutions depend on external sources of funding to support their academic support systems, it is only a short-term solution to providing effective academic support. First, these resources are becoming less available and more difficult to obtain. More importantly, they are really a Band-Aid approach to providing support. They exist for prescribed amounts of time and are based on evaluation criteria that do not really inform the institution of how to improve their own internal systems. They provide a quantitative lens that is a part of the picture but often does not take into consideration the challenge of going beyond academic skills discussed in recommendation two.

With a reliance on external funding, the core faculty and other significant institutional units are often uninformed about the support, which can leave both the students who are eligible to access its resources and its staff marginalized from the core of the institution. These support systems are frequently designed by staff hired specifically under the criteria of the grant and are often not at the table when decisions are made regarding institutional mission and purpose. Their accountability is to an authority beyond the institution and is often regarded simply as a source of funding and not as an integrated part of the whole.

When the support system is built into the basic budget of the institution, a core administrator is responsible for its management and is also held accountable to the same standards of performance as others across the school. It undergoes the same review process as all other programs across the institution ensuring that it is on a level playing field with other academic initiatives. The program is also more likely to be integrated into the overall mission because the core administrator responsible for managing it is at the table when strategic planning is taking place. This can ensure a more permanent position within the school, increased visibility and commitment, and also a level of responsiveness to ongoing changes and student demographics equal to other units.

Action Step: Build Academic Support into Institutional Strategic Planning

This step is a logical outcome of decreasing dependence on external funding. If the institution makes a commitment to build academic support into its basic budget, it should follow that academic support will be part of the strategic planning process. The manager responsible for the support unit, being accountable for its outcomes, needs to be at the table when strategic planning is taking place at the institutional level.

Strategic planning involves setting goals related to the institution's mission and purpose and working collaboratively across units to determine how to meet them. It usually involves reflecting on past goals and current programs and reviewing data that informs the decision makers how to build on institutional successes, revise or eliminate problem areas, and meet the ever-changing needs of the marketplace. The decision makers usually include administrators from academic as well as nonacademic units. Consequently, deans are describing their programs; enrollment and marketing vice presidents are reviewing challenges related to recruitment; and chief financial officers are talking about budget constraints. If the academic support system is not represented in this very significant discussion, it can easily be forgotten and the institution may lose an important component that provides linkages across these units. For example, without academic support there may be academic programs that do not attract students due to a challenging curriculum and a lack of perceived assistance; with academic support, the programs may seem more accessible, generate more enrollment and, consequently, more revenue. Without academic support, enrollment loses a recruitment tool; with academic support, marketing can be enhanced by touting the institution's commitment to helping students to succeed and meet their goals. Without academic support, the university may lose revenue as students fail to persist and drop out; with academic support, students are more likely to persist to graduation, leading the institution to generate additional revenue.

Recommendation Four: Develop a Reward System That Values Teaching

Faculty success in academia, specifically with four-year institutions, has traditionally been measured by the ability to publish, make presentations that contribute to the professional field, and carry out research. Opportunities for promotion, tenure, or salary increase are heavily based on these criteria. While these institutions claim that they value teaching, these faculty members spend fewer hours in the classroom and in advising than those who teach at community colleges. Additionally, the weight and importance that teaching carries in the promotion and tenure process is usually far less than publishing and research, and criteria for tenure and promotion have not changed significantly over the years. Most four-year institutions also receive endowments that reward research rather than excellence in teaching; not rewarding these efforts sends a clear message as to what is most highly valued within the institution.

On the other hand, two-year institutions, specifically community colleges, place a greater emphasis on the role of teaching than do four-year institutions. In the past, community college faculty were required to have earned at least a master's degree, however, expectations are changing as positions in four-year institutions become harder to find. This dearth of positions at four-year institutions means increased competition for community college positions, resulting in a larger pool of applicants with PhDs, so more community colleges are requiring a doctoral degree. The upside of this practice means community colleges have a larger pool of highly educated applicants to choose from. Additionally, these PhDs may really prefer teaching as their primary responsibility.

They are expected, as are faculty at four-year institutions, to participate in activities that fall under the category of "service to the community." There is seldom the pressure to publish or carry out research. While publishing and research play a lesser role, in some two-year institutions, faculty is expected to publish and conduct research. This is in addition to maintaining office hours, which often exceed 10–12 hours a week.

Since the mission of community colleges is to educate all constituents, entrance requirements are seldom stringent, and faculty works with a greater proportion of academically underprepared students than those at most four-year institutions. Consequently, a large part of their teaching responsibilities include a substantial role in the provision of academic assistance. For those faculty who teach an underprepared population *and* are pressured to publish, this can be truly overwhelming.

The concept of valuing teaching and advising at four-year institutions represents a significant change in institutional culture; if increased importance is placed on teaching, then a greater emphasis may be placed on faculty to take a more active role in advising and teaching first-year students. This development may not be very appealing to researchers and potential new faculty. Along with the changing population entering institutions comes risk, fear, and misconceptions. Faculty may be unwilling to rethink their delivery and may perhaps need opportunities to discuss changes in philosophy to look at what impedes development.

*Action Step: Faculty Development Should Include Opportunities
to Refine and Develop Instructional Strategies*

In order for faculty to grow and develop, an institution must be open to change. It is important to think of faculty as valuable resources and experts in their fields who should take the lead in the development of their course content and instructional strategies. Since they are on the front lines, faculty knows what works within the classroom and what does not. Offering released time or stipends to faculty who take the lead in fostering best practices would be one way for an institution to show it values teaching.

Offering a series of "faculty share" workshops could be another way to celebrate the faculty who develop and implement best practices in their classrooms. We constantly tell our students that they can learn much from each other, but we seem to forget that about ourselves as teachers. A faculty share workshop could offer ongoing and frequent opportunities for conversations about instructional strategies; what is working in the classroom and what is not. At one college, for example, faculty members have raised concerns over the increase in plagiarism in homework assignments. Another group had concerns about how to deal with problem students in online courses. Based on these concerns, the college decided to host a series of informal "Brown Bag Lunches" to discuss these issues and possible resolutions or interventions.

Faculty might also poll their colleagues as to what they would like to see for development and teaching needs. Based on that, they might create a teaching evaluation handbook with ongoing opportunities for teacher self-reflection. Workshops might be offered based on the result of the poll within and outside the departments. Visiting colleagues' classrooms, collaborating with community college colleagues, and getting a firm commitment from the institution to ensure monies for travel to conferences/workshops related to teaching are additional ways in which faculty can be supported and encouraged to continue honing their practice.

Efforts to recognize and reward faculty must also include an often overlooked and overworked constituency: adjunct faculty. More often than not, adjuncts hired at the last minute, without a formal search, form a disproportional number of those who teach undergraduate students. Hired only if the classes fill, they are often given a syllabus, a book, and a class list, and sent on their way. Undergraduate classes and especially noncredit or university-credit-only courses are staffed by a disproportional number of adjunct faculty. Often they are called at the last minute, given a class list, a syllabus, and a room number. Adjuncts are seldom invited to join in the talks on policy or asked for input regarding delivery and are usually given courses that senior faculty prefer not to teach. They are generally not asked for their input on course content, delivery methods, or teaching materials and have limited, if any, opportunities to develop and enhance their teaching strategies and to provide academic support to their students.

Opportunities for adjunct faculty development could take the form of a mentoring or buddy system: senior full-time faculty paired with an adjunct. At some institutions adjunct faculty are invited to participate in all faculty development efforts and are often given a stipend for participating.

Action Step: Develop an Institution-Wide System of Faculty Evaluation

The subject of faculty evaluation is a prickly one. Who should do it? Who should develop the criteria by which they are evaluated? What should it look like? In order for changes to happen, an institution must have a clear vision of what it wants to achieve regarding evaluation. It is necessary, first, to create a climate of accountability. An institution can do this through the development of an institution-wide system of evaluation and criteria, with clear descriptions of faculty responsibilities that would respond to needed reforms in teaching practices.

Most institutions provide a generic form at the end of the term for students to evaluate the teacher, the course, the materials, and delivery. The form itself must also be evaluated to make it meaningful. Who should develop this form? Do the questions asked actually correspond to what is taking place in the classroom? Is the same form used for all courses, despite differences in content, delivery, and course length? When are students given the opportunity to respond to the evaluation?

Frequently, evaluations are given at the end of the term, on the last day of class, during the last 10 minutes or so. Students at this point, just wanting to be done with it all, race through the categories checking boxes with little thought to what they are doing. Over the years, term after term, we have heard students complain about having to fill out course evaluations. We hear comments like: "I'm not going to say anything bad. I might have this teacher again," "Why do we have to do this every term? No one reads these anyway, and if they do, no one does anything about them." "It's too late for this to benefit me." While there are usually places for students to write comments, few do so. The process then becomes meaningless, an exercise in futility.

If the evaluations were actually completed with reflection and honesty, they could be valuable resources with a significant role in informing one's practice. So how do we make this a more meaningful experience for students and faculty?

One thought is to provide the evaluation instrument on the first day of class, rather than the last, when students are ready to bolt out of the door. If it is discussed up front, the faculty can educate students as to the importance of teaching evaluations, and how this feedback can truly help the faculty evaluate their own practice and make ongoing improvements in content and delivery. If the students are reminded to periodically look at and think about evaluation as an ongoing part of the course, there may be a change in the way students' value the process. Educating students how to assess teaching and how to negotiate evaluation forms is essential to obtaining meaningful feedback.

From the institutions' end, responsibility needs to be taken to disseminate the information garnered from the evaluations and to take some action. Are there trends that keep appearing? Do faculty need additional development opportunities in order to improve delivery methods? Are certain faculty members receiving rave reviews term after term? Here is an opportunity for the institution to really use its faculty as resources, as mentors, to be consulted with an effort to support all faculty across the institution.

Faculty, including adjuncts, should be identified and rewarded for excellence in teaching from criteria developed by a council of peers. It is also time to expand criteria for promotion and tenure to include a greater emphasis on pedagogy. Criteria for promotion and tenure should be modified to reflect excellence in teaching as well as to emphasize and value the role of undergraduate teaching.

Roueche, Ely, and Roueche (2001) suggest that faculty recognition might come in the form of a "Celebration of Faculty," with recognition of all those nominated for excellence. Some of the categories for awards they describe honor both full- and part-time faculty. Categories could be "faculty of the year," voted on by peers, "the recognition and celebration of all faculty" and "recognition of faculty advising excellence," as well as "spontaneous recognition for jobs well done" (p. 95–97).

Institutions can show they value teaching in many ways. For instance, when making new hires, an institution can ensure linkage to mission and teaching emphasis. Another way would be to create different tracks for faculty, such as a track with a teaching focus and one with a research focus, that hold equal status within the institution.

An institution can also seek funding and grants to recognize and reward faculty, improve teaching and the development of new resources, and identify and disseminate information on sources of funding for teaching innovations that influence teaching and learning.

Institutional funds can also be made available for "Excellence in Teaching" initiatives and can come in the form of one-time bonuses; these rewards could also be in the form of increased faculty development funds, released time, institution-wide recognition, and "pay for performance." It is important, too, that the institutions ensure that awards for teaching are comparable to those for research and scholarship.

Recommendation Five: Develop a Culture of Evidence

An interesting aspect of higher education, and actually education in general, is its reluctance to create sets of evaluative data that go beyond standardized and quantitative measures and really inform its practice. In higher education, colleges and universities are very cognizant of the need for accreditation; this is what keeps them in business, and they must pay close attention to the criteria set forth by regional and professional accrediting agencies. Too often, however, the institution will wait for the agency's scheduled review visit, which could be every ten years, before it takes a look at whether or not it is making progress toward its mission. To prepare for these critical reviews, institutional teams are formed to conduct and write a self-assessment report. Evaluation data are collected, which are based on external criteria set by the accrediting agency and are generally summative in nature. That is to say, the data are frequently not collected or used along the way to help the institution do a better job of educating its students. The typical accreditation process involves compiling the self-assessment document followed by an external peer review team visit to the institution, which then produces a written response to the institutional document. The emphasis is on following the process accurately, and too often the self-assessment document, which takes an extraordinary amount of time to compile, ends up sitting on a shelf following the review.

According to an institutional survey undertaken by Roueche, Ely, and Roueche,

> The majority of colleges were not collecting data that would tell them, in fact, if they were fulfilling their mission ... We concluded that colleges did not understand how to link mission to effectiveness measures, were not inclined to do so, or had not thought of it (2001).

Indeed, the traditional accreditation process rewards those institutions that simply replicate the process that is utilized across all institutions.

To develop a culture of evidence means going beyond data collection that is exclusively quantitative and standardized across institutions. It means constructing objectives and tangible outcomes that are tied to the mission and purpose of the institution and determining, using the data, on a regular basis whether or not they are being met. If they are not being met, then the educational practice must be revised based on what the data show. Everyone across the institution must be actively engaged in the routine collection of informative data, and there must be an expectation that a regular assessment of how their unit is meeting expectations is being undertaken. This expectation begins with the president and the Board of Trustees and involves all units, both academic and nonacademic.

The Higher Learning Commission has recently developed an alternative route to accreditation that moves the process away from one of compliance to one of continuous improvement. By engaging in this innovative procedure (Academic Quality Improvement Program, AQIP), self-assessment becomes a living document that truly serves as a tool for ongoing reflection and revision. In order to participate in AQIP, an institution is required to conduct a preliminary self-assessment that provides evidence that it sees itself "as a set of systems and processes, rather than as a collection of offices, departments, and academic or administrative units" (Handbook of Accreditation 2003, p. 6:1–2). This is a significant step forward toward creating a culture of evidence, which allows all stakeholders, internal to the institution as well as the general public, to really understand if the institution is making a difference and what outcomes are expected.

Action Step: Build a Comprehensive System of Assessment

As we stated earlier, assessment cannot simply be an add-on that takes place at the end of an activity to signal its end. It is a cycle that begins as soon as a potential student inquires about an institution and continues throughout their enrollment and into their postgraduation years as alumni. If the data is informative, stakeholders will examine it regularly for the story it tells them about how effectively they are doing their jobs and at what points they need to consider change.

To look at a micro example of this formative and cyclical nature of assessment, let us consider a hypothetical classroom experience. At the start of a course, the instructor assesses the students' level of expertise in the course content area. Once she has determined the range of expertise in the class, she can adjust the pace and perhaps the amount of content she will try to cover. Along the way, she continuously administers a range of evaluation measures to make sure the students are learning and where their confusions may lie. This allows her to once again adjust her pace and review the content to ensure understanding. At times throughout the course she may ask the students to write a short paper on the material covered to see if they are getting the big picture, and at other times, she may administer a quick multiple-choice test to see if they are picking up the details. By the end of the course, she has a pretty good understanding of where the students are in terms of grasping the material. This all occurs before the end-of-course grades, which would only allow her to see, after the fact, how the students performed on a final test or project. The final grade will have limited value and will only indicate to the instructor the range of understanding at the end. It will not tell her where the understanding broke down or help her make a difference in student outcomes. It provides a very limited and not particularly informative set of data to both the students and the instructor.

This same concept can be applied at the institutional level. What data are being collected along the way to assess the systems designed to support students and their learning outcomes? How are the data used to inform institutional practice and help decision makers ensure best practice? Who has access to the data as it is gathered? If institutions wait until students are ready to graduate to collect data and continue to emphasize summative, quantitative measures, they will have a difficult time proving that they have a meaningful system of evaluation. It is analogous to the instructor who only looks at final course grades to evaluate student learning; who is accountable if half the students fail? How does the instructor know where to change the learning environment to ensure more passing grades next time? Likewise, if the institution discovers that its graduation rate is only 35 percent, who is accountable? How does it know where to change the learning environment to ensure higher graduation rates?

Action Step: Disseminate Data Widely and Publicly to All Stakeholders

In order to create and maintain a culture that integrates assessment and evaluation across all units, data must be shared with everyone involved. Within the institution, in order to create trust and lessen any anxiety that may be tied to assessment, data needs to be shared, and it also needs to be clear that decisions are made based on the data rather than informal anecdotes describing program effectiveness. If all units are expected to share their data and be held accountable for it, those responsible will be more vigilant about collecting relevant information and organizing it to show how it is used. The decision-making process must be transparent and directly linked to the data. For example, if academic programs are asked to report on their student persistence rates, the enrollment/recruiting unit should be asked to report how many inquiries convert to student enrollments, and both units should have access to the two sets of data. By looking at enrollment conversion rates and comparing them to rates of persistence, the two units might start discussing whether or not recruiters are describing accurately the fit between an incoming student and the program. They may find that there was not a good fit from the start, which is leading to increased dropouts.

In addition to creating an internal culture of evidence, there are external stakeholders who also should have access to reports detailing clearly the effectiveness of an institution and how it relates to the institutional mission. For public institutions, taxpayers want to see data that confirm for them that the institution is doing its job. For legislators and funding agencies, it is imperative that when monies become available there is a record of institutional outcome measures so they do not have to take the time to hunt for the information. It should be already well known to them what an institution is doing well. Also, if a legislative bill comes to the floor of the House or Senate and a university representative is asked to testify on its behalf, there needs to be an immediate source of data to inform the testimony.

At private institutions, the Board of Trustees needs ready access to relevant data in order to make informed decisions and also to support fund-raising activities. Boards are usually composed of individuals who have little time to read volumes of data, so it is also vital to have it summarized and clearly organized with little educational jargon.

Action Step: Provide Evidence That Encourages Funding for a More Seamless System of Education across All Levels

Once an institution has established a climate of regular, informative data gathering, it is important to look across the traditional barricades that have existed for years among educational levels and to partner to create more streamlined systems for students. This means that high schools, community colleges, and four-year institutions collaborate on educational activities designed to set expectations for sixteen years of education at an earlier stage and to create support systems to facilitate more dynamic working relationships.

We discussed earlier the need to develop such seamless programs, but we want to underscore in this section the importance of evaluating their effectiveness by collecting and organizing longitudinal sets of data. Without the data demonstrating the long-term outcomes from such programs, there will be little opportunity to obtain funding for them and most likely they will suffer cutbacks. Participants need to anticipate this funding need from the start and build in a regular cycle of assessment.

A FINAL WORD

In this final chapter, we have made five overall recommendations along with sixteen action steps that we believe can enhance access to higher education and ensure that it is meaningful for everyone across different types of institutions. While not intended to be inclusive, our list is offered in the spirit of extending the conversation that was started in this oral history. We urge the reader to reflect on what these storytellers had to share and how this partial history of American education can provide insight for the future.

❧ INTERVIEWEE BIOGRAPHIES

DAVID ARENDALE is an associate professor at the General College of the University of Minnesota. He has contributed to the field of developmental education in multiple ways, including serving as president of NADE, and writing articles on the history of the field and supplemental instruction.

JUELE BLANKENBERG is a retired manager of tutoring services at Oakton Community College in Illinois. She frequently teaches as an adjunct in the Adult, Continuing, and Literacy Education graduate program at National-Louis University in Chicago, Illinois.

NANCY BORNSTEIN is the director of the Learning Center at Alverno College, a private four-year, liberal arts, Catholic college for women, in Milwaukee, Wisconsin. She has been active in the field of learning assistance—serving as vice president, president, and past-president of NCLCA (1989–1992), an invited participant in Future Directions in Developmental Education (2001, 2003), a consultant to other programs, and most recently, coeditor of the *Learning Assistance Review.*

HUNTER R. BOYLAN is the director of the Center for Developmental Education at Appalachian State University and the director of the Kellogg Institute. He has conducted nationally recognized research studies related to models for student success and authored many publications on the topic, including, most recently, *What Works: Research-Based Best Practices in Developmental Education.*

SONIA BUCKNER, age thirty-seven, is a former developmental student and a graduate of Alverno College, a four-year, liberal arts, private, Catholic, women's college in Milwaukee, Wisconsin. She currently works as a police officer, but is looking forward to continue her education so that she might change her career path.

SUSAN CLARKE-THAYER, associate dean of the College of Arts and Sciences at Suffolk University in Boston, Massachusetts, started her career as a reading specialist. She was instrumental in developing standards for best practice, and edited *NADE Self-Evaluation Guides.*

THELMA COLEMAN is a former developmental student, currently working as an administrative coordinator for the Center for Academic Development at National-Louis University. Thelma has also received her MA in human services from National-Louis University.

K. PATRICIA CROSS is professor emeritus of higher education at the University of California, Berkeley. She wrote *Accent on Learning* in 1976, and *Beyond the Open Door* in 1971. She held a joint appointment with the Center for Research and Development in Higher Education and the Center for Educational Testing Service, both in Berkeley.

TIANA ELLIS, a former developmental student at Olive Harvey City College of Chicago, has completed a law degree and has recently passed the Illinois State Bar Exam.

DAWN HARRINGTON, age thirty-one, is a former developmental student. She received her BA in English and social science. Ms. Harrington is an administrative assistant for the School of Education at National-Louis University.

JEANNE L. HIGBEE is a professor and faculty chair in the General College at the University of Minnesota. She has written numerous articles and is an editor for the *CRDEUL* monograph series, as well as coeditor for the *Learning Assistance Review.*

DANA BRITT LUNDELL directs the Center for Research on Developmental Education and Urban Literacy at the University of Minnesota's General College. Author of numerous articles, Dr. Lundell also coedits the *CRDEUL* monograph series, and manages multiple research activities.

CALVIN MACKIE, a former developmental student, is now an associate professor of mechanical engineering at Tulane University. He is the 2004 winner of the NADE Distinguished Alumnus of a Developmental Education Program.

MARTHA MAXWELL is truly a pioneer in the area of student support. She founded reading- and study-skills centers at American University and the University of Maryland. She has mentored hundreds, if not thousands, of professionals and has authored multiple books and articles that have become classics. Maxwell received her BA degree in 1946 and her doctorate in 1960 at the University of Maryland. She is most well known for her seminal publication, *Improving Student Learning Skills*, published in 1979.

ROBERT McCABE served as president of Miami-Dade Community College, and led the college through a major reform movement in the 1980s. His important book, *No One to Waste*, which concludes with policy recommendations, is an excellent example of his ongoing commitment to the underprepared student. He has also produced a video, for boards of trustees, dealing with why there are underprepared students.

NADEGE MEYER, former developmental student, was a graduate student in the Adult and Continuing Literacy Program at National-Louis University in Illinois. Ms. Meyer has since stopped out to raise her new baby.

JANE NEUBURGER is the director of the Learning Resource Center at Syracuse University. Neuberger has been influential in setting standards for exemplary practice, and chairs the NADE Certification Council for the National Association for Developmental Education.

KAREN PATTY-GRAHAM, director of Instructional Services at Southern Illinois University, has served in many leadership roles including vice president of NADE. She is also a NADE Certification Council reviewer.

GAIL PLATT is the director of the Learning Center at South Plains College in Texas and has been active in professional organizations.

NASRIN RAHMANI, originally from Iran, is a former developmental student, who holds a BA degree from National-Louis University and has recently begun her graduate studies.

ROBIN REMICH is the manager of the Learning Center at Oakton Community College/Ray Hartstein Campus (RHC) and oversees the Comprehensive Tutoring Program, Testing Center, Services for Students with Disabilities, and Student Support Services/TRIO. Robin is currently working on her dissertation at Loyola University, in the Higher Education Program in the Department of Educational Leadership. She has worked in the field of education for twenty years.

LOLA ROMERO received her GED after being out of school for thirty-seven years and currently works in the Radiology Department at a university medical center. She is currently enrolled in a BA program, and she is working toward a degree in radiology.

MIKE ROSE has authored numerous articles and books, including *Lives on the Boundary* and *Possible Lives*. He holds a PhD in educational psychology and is on the faculty of the UCLA Graduate School of Education and Information Studies and UCLA Writing Programs.

GARY SARETSKY is the founder and first president of the National Association for Developmental Education and project director for the Improvement of PostSecondary Education. He is currently the senior marketing director for Practice Builders.

GLADYS SHAW is a retired director of the Tutoring and Learning Center and currently is the program director for Student Support Services at the University of Texas at El Paso. She has been actively involved in setting national standards for tutors and academic support services in colleges and universities. Gladys was recently elected a Fellow by the

American Council for Developmental Education, the profession's highest honor.

SANTIAGO SILVA, at the time of the interview, was the vice president for Student Services and Development at South Texas Community College and has served as an officer in multiple professional associations related to helping students succeed in college. Dr. Silva was recently nominated for a Fellows Leadership Program sponsored by the Hispanic Association for Colleges and Universities (HACU).

SHARON SILVERMAN is the former director of the Learning Assistance Center and has taught in the School of Education at Loyola University. She currently teaches in the Adult, Continuing and Literacy Education graduate program at National-Louis University in Chicago, and works as an educational consultant in higher education. Dr. Silverman was also a Fulbright Senior Scholar in South Africa during the 1999 academic year. She is the coauthor of *Learning and Development* and *Learning Assistance and Developmental Education*.

MILTON "BUNK" SPANN served as the first director of the National Center for Developmental Education at Appalachian State University. He was the founding editor of the *Journal of Developmental and Remedial Education*, currently known as the *Journal of Developmental Education*, where he is now editor emeritus. Retired as a practitioner, he has over thirty years of experience in the field of developmental education.

DAVID V. TAYLOR was the dean of the General College at the University of Minnesota at the time of the interview. He has been active professionally in the community, looking at early interventions to support disadvantaged youth. Dr. Taylor has since accepted a position as provost at Morehouse College in Atlanta. Additionally, he will be senior vice president for Academic Affairs and chief operations officer for Morehouse.

TAMU WRIGHT, age thirty-three, is a former developmental student and is currently taking courses at Olive Harvey City College of Chicago, in addition to raising her family. She works as a teacher assistant at Dunne Academy, and plans to continue her higher education.

 # GLOSSARY

Access Programs—Programs committed to providing access to institutions of higher education to underrepresented populations.

ACT—American College Test.

APA—American Psychological Association.

Articulation Agreement—An agreement between participating institutions, designed to allow students to transfer lower-division general-education coursework from one school to another.

Astin's Talent Development Perspective—"Astin's (1990) view that program quality in higher education should be defined as the talent development of every student, rather than the average SAT score of entering classes or the percentage of seniors going on to graduate school. From this talent development perspective, the criterion defining quality is the extent to which each student (regardless of conventional disability/ability status) develops the target knowledge and skills established by the college curriculum" (Porter 1994).

Bridge Program—Similar to Freshman Experience Program. Structured courses/programs taught in a cooperative environment between instructors to support newly admitted students.

College Assistance Migrant Program (CAMP)—"CAMP assists students who are migratory or seasonal farmworkers (or children of such workers) enrolled in their first year of undergraduate studies at an institution of higher education." http://www.ed.gov/programs/camp/index.html

Compensatory—Compensatory programs are designed to "compensate" for what is lacking in the cultural and linguistic backgrounds of "at risk" students.

Criterion-Referenced Grading—Grading that measures student performance against defined criteria. Often used to ensure that as many students as possible who successfully meet the criteria may achieve As.

CRLA—College Reading and Learning Association is an association for post-secondary learning assistance professionals. http://www.crla.net/

Developmental—A term first used in education in the 1970s that replaced the more negative connotations of "remedial" and "compensatory." Developmental programs take a comprehensive view of the individual student to enhance both academic and personal areas (Casazza & Silverman 1996).

ESL—English as a Second Language.

First-Year Experience Program—A structured program that provides resources to promote a successful first year of college.

Freshman Experience Program—Same as First Year Experience Program.

GED—General Equivalency Diploma. The GED Tests measure a candidate's knowledge and academic skills against those of today's traditional high school graduates. http://www.acenet.edu/AM/Template.cfm?Section=GEDTS

GI Bill—The Servicemen's Readjustment Act of 1944, better known as the GI Bill of Rights, was first passed in 1944. This legislation provides benefits for those who have served in the U.S. armed forces.

GPA—Grade Point Average.

HeadStart—Longest-running national school-readiness program in the United States.

HELP Program—The HELP (Higher Education for Low-income People) Center was started in 1967 at University of Minnesota's General College to serve educationally and academically disadvantaged students, including students of color and student-parents.

Holistic—When used in education, this term means considering the "whole students" in providing academic support.

HomeStart—The UK's leading family support group organization. It provides support to families through home visits, groups, and social events. http://www.home-start.org.uk/site/aboutus.html

Learning Assistance—Academic support provided through services such as tutoring, workshops, supplemental instruction, academic counseling, and ADA accommodations.

Locus of Control—A term used in social learning theory to refer to the belief that one can control internal and external factors to influence outcomes of personal goals (Silverman & Casazza 2000).

MLA—Modern Language Association.

NADE—National Association for Developmental Education.

National Merit Scholar—An academic competition for scholarships, started in 1955.

NCLCA—The National College Learning Center Association is an organization of professionals dedicated to promoting excellence among learning-center personnel. http://www.nclca.org/

NEA—"The National Education Association—the nation's largest professional employee organization—committed to advancing the cause of public education." http://www.nea.org/aboutnea/index.html

No Child Left Behind Act—An educational reform passed by President Bush in 2002 that focuses on accountability for results, parental choice, and scientifically proven instructional methods. http://www.ed.gov/index.jhtml

Reality Counseling—A method of counseling that focuses on helping individuals take responsibility for their actions and behaviors.

Remedial—In education, the term focuses on correcting specific skill deficits in students. Although still used in elementary and secondary curriculum, this term, in higher education, has been replaced with the term "developmental."

SAT—Scholastic Aptitude Test.

Social promotion—The practice of promoting students to the next level, to keep them with their peers, regardless of their academic capabilities.

START Program (formerly the Provisional Admission Program)—A form of provisional admission whereby "students must attend orientation, must be advised by the Academic Advising Center, must select their classes from a list of prescribed university courses, and must take a free, noncredit study skills course" (University of Texas at El Paso Undergraduate Catalog http://www.utep.edu/catalogs/undergrad/).

Supplemental Instruction (SI)—A national academic support program that provides academic support facilitated by peer tutors, or "SI Leaders."

Talent Search—"Programs that provide academic, career, and financial counseling to students from disadvantaged backgrounds and encourage them to graduate from high school and continue on to the postsecondary school of their choice." http://www.ed.gov/programs/triotalent/index.html

Texas Academic Skills Program (TASP)—"The Texas Academic Skills Program (TASP®) is an instructional program designed to ensure that students attending public institutions of higher learning in Texas and students entering educator preparation programs in Texas have the academic skills necessary to perform effectively in college-level work. Students not yet proficient in an academic area are required to participate in developmental education activities." http://www.tasp.nesinc.com/index.htm

Tracking—Grouping students in the classroom or in programs based on ability levels.

TRIO—"Federal funded programs targeting students from disadvantaged backgrounds. Federal Trio Programs include five separate programs: Upward Bound, Talent Search, Student Support Services, Educational Opportunity Centers, and the Upward Bound Math/Science program." http://www.ed.gov/about/offices/list/ope/trio/index.html

Upward Bound Program—"A program that provides support for the preparation for college entrance, serving high school students from low-income families." http://www.ed.gov/programs/trioupbound/index.html

✒ REFERENCES

Abraham, A. A. & Creech, J. D. (2000). *Reducing remedial education: What progress are the states making?* Southern Regional Education Board Report.

Adelman, C. (2005). *Moving into town—and moving on: The community college in the lives of traditional-age students.* Washington, DC: U.S. Department of Education.

Arendale, D. (2002). History of Supplemental (SI): Mainstreaming of developmental education. In Dana Britt Lundell and Jeanne Higbee (eds.), *Histories of Developmental Education.* Minneapolis: University of Minnesota, Center for Research and Developmental Education and Urban Literacy.

Bandura, A. (1977). Self-efficacy: Toward a unifying theory of behavior change. *Psychological Review,* 84: 191–215.

———. (1982). Self-efficacy mechanism in human agency. *American Psychologist,* 37: 122–147.

———. (1986). *Social foundations of thought and action: A social cognitive theory.* Englewood Cliffs, NJ: Prentice Hall.

———. (1997). *Self-efficacy: The exercise of control.* New York: Freeman.

Barbe, W. (1951). Reading-improvement services in colleges and universities. *School and Society,* 74(1907): 6–7.

Book, W. F. (1927). Educational research and statistics: How well college students can read. *School and Society,* 26(660): 242–248.

Boylan, H. R. (2002). *What works: A guide to research-based best practices in developmental education.* A joint project of the Continuous Quality Improvement Network and the National Center for Developmental Education.

Brier, E. (1984). Bridging the academic preparation gap: An historical view. *Journal of Developmental Education,* 8: 2–5.

Brubacher, J. S., & Rudy, W. (1976). *Higher educational transition: A history of American colleges and universities 1636–1976* (3rd ed.). New York: HarperCollins.

Butts, R. F., & Cremin, L. A. (1953). *A history of education in American culture*. Troy, MO: Rinehart & Winston.

Carnegie Foundation for the Advancement of Teaching. (1973). *Priorities for action: Final report of the Carnegie Commission on Higher Education*. New York: McGraw-Hill.

Casazza, M. E., & Silverman, S. L. (1996). *Learning assistance and developmental education*. San Francisco: Jossey-Bass.

Clowes, D. A. (1980). More than a definitional problem: Remedial, compensatory, and developmental education. *Journal of Developmental and Remedial Education*, 4(1): 8–10.

Cohen, A. M., & Brawer, F. B. (1982). *The American community college*. San Francisco: Jossey-Bass.

Collins, T. (2002). Foreword. In Dana Britt Lundell and Jeanne Higbee (eds.), *Histories of Developmental Education*. Minneapolis: University of Minnesota, Center for Research on Developmental Education and Urban Literacy.

Cross, K. P. (1971). *Beyond the open door: New students to higher education*. San Francisco: Jossey-Bass.

―――. (1976). *Accent on learning*. San Francisco: Jossey-Bass.

Eliot, C. W. (1969). *American education: Its men, ideas and institutions*. New York: Arno Press and New York Times.

Federal Student Assistance. (n.d.). *Finding out about financial aid*. Retrieved June 1, 2005 from http://www.ed.gov/officesOSFAP/Students/student.html.

Gleazer, E. J. J. (Winter 1970). The community college issue of the 1970s. *Educational Record*, 47–52.

Greenburg. (2004). *Chronicle of Higher Education*, 50(40): B9.

Hardin, C. J. (1988). Access to higher education: Who belongs? *Journal of Developmental Education*, 12(1): 2–4, 6, 19.

Higher Learning Commission. (2003). Handbook of accreditation (3rd ed.). Chicago, 6: 1–2.

Honawar, V. (2005). Community colleges are serving more younger adults, report says. *Education Week*, 24(27): 10–11.

Keimig, R. T. (1983). *Raising academic standards: A guide to learning improvement*. (ASHE-ERIC Higher Education Rep. No. 4). Washington, DC: Association for the Study of Higher Education.

King, R. C. (1985). The changing student. *National Forum*, 65: 22–27.

Lavin, D. E., Alba, R. D., & Silberstein, R. A. (1981). *Right versus privilege: The open-admissions experiment at the city university of New York*. New York: Free Press.

Maxwell, M. (1979). *Improving student learning skills*. San Francisco: Jossey-Bass.

McCabe, R.H. (1983). Miami-Dade results justify program. *Community and Junior College Journal*, 54(1): 26–29.

———. (2000). *No one to waste: A report to public decision-makers and community leaders*. Washington, DC: Community College Press.

Minneapolis City Council Resolution. (2005). E-mail message dated April 15, 2005 from GC Communications. Retrieved on April 20, 2005 from gccommunications@tc.umn.edu.

Moore, W. (1971). *Blind man on a freeway: The community college administrator*. London: Jossey-Bass.

National Association for Developmental Education. (Revised July 31, 1998). *Need for developmental education at four-year institutions*. Retrieved from http://www.umkc.edu/cad/nade/nadedocs/psde4y98.htm.

National Committee of Inquiry into Higher Education. (1997). *Higher education in the learning society* (Dearing Report). London: HMSO, p. 128.

Parr, F. W. (1930). The extent of remedial reading work in state universities in the United States. *School and Society*, 31(799): 547–548.

Rose, M. (1989). *Lives on the boundary: The struggles and achievements of America's underprepared*. New York: Free Press.

———. (1995). *Possible lives: The promise of public education in America*. New York: Penguin.

Roueche, J. E., & Roueche, S. D. (1999). *High stakes, high performance: Making remedial education work*. Washington, DC: Community College Press.

Roueche, J. E., Baker, G., & Roueche, S. D. (1984). *College responses to low-achieving students*. New York: Harcourt, Brace, and Jovanovich.

Roueche, J. E., Ely, E. E., & Roueche, S. D. (2001). *In pursuit of excellence*. Washington, DC: Community College Press.

Rubin, M. (1991). A glossary of developmental education terms compiled by the CRLA task force on professional language for college reading and learning. *Journal of College Reading and Learning*, 23(1): 1–13.

Shaw, M. E. (2002). Recovering the vision of John Dewey for developmental education. In Dana Britt Lundell and Jeanne Higbee (eds.), *Histories of developmental education*, p. 32. Minneapolis: University of Minnesota, The Center for Research on Developmental Education and Urban Literacy.

Silverman, S. L., & Casazza, M. E. (2000). *Learning and development: Making connections to enhance teaching*. San Francisco: Jossey-Bass.

Svinicki, M. D. (Spring 1991). Practical implications of cognitive theories. *New Directions for Teaching and Learning*, 45: 27–37.

Taylor, D. V. (2002). Supporting the research mission. In Dana Britt Lundell and Jeanne Higbee (eds.), *Histories of developmental education*, p. 8. Minneapolis:

University of Minnesota, The Center for Research on Developmental Education and Urban Literacy.

——. (2005). *As a matter of principle.* Retrieved May 2, 2005 from http://www.gen.umn.edu/gc/DVT_aMoP.htm.

Tomlinson, L. M. (1989). *Postsecondary developmental programs* (Rep. No. 3). Washington, DC: School of Education and Human Development, George Washington University.

Traub, J. (1994). *City on a hill: Testing the American dream at city college.* New York: Addison-Wesley.

Weidner, H. Z. (1990). Back to the future. Paper presented at the Conference on College Composition and Communication, Chicago.

Weinstein, C. E. (1982). *A metacurriculum for remediating learning-strategies deficits in academically underprepared students.* Iowa City: American College Testing Service, National Center for Advancing Educational Practice.

Wyatt, M. (1992). The past, present, and future need for college reading courses in the U.S. *Journal of Reading,* 36(1): 10–20.

Zimmerman, B. J. (1990). Self-regulated learning and academic achievement: An overview. *Educational Psychologist,* 25(1): 2–17.

✎ INDEX

ABOUT THE AUTHORS

MARTHA E. CASAZZA is Dean at the College of Arts and Sciences, Louis-National University in Chicago. Dr. Casazza has authored two books with Dr. Sharon Silverman: *Learning Assistance and Developmental Education: A Guide for Effective Practice* (1966) and *Learning and Development* (2000). She served as President of the National College Learning Center Association for Developmental Education and is currently on the Editorial Board for the Journal of Developmental Education. Dr. Casazza received the Hunter R. Boylan Outstanding Research Research/Publication Award.

LAURA BAUER is the Blended Program Director in the Department of Adult and Continuing Literacy Education. She also directs the Undergraduate Developmental Studies Program. Dr. Bauer was selected as one of two featured developmental educators in the PBS/Starlink Broadcast, "Developmental Education: Policy and Pedagogy." She is working on a textbook, "Reading for College, Reading for Life," with Linda Sweeney, for Bedford/St. Martin Press.